PROVIDORE

pro

SIMON JOHNSON

vidore

HODDER

A Hodder Book

First published in 1999
by Hodder Headline Australia Pty Limited
(A member of the Hodder Headline Group)
Level 22, 201 Kent Street, Sydney NSW 2000
Website: www.hha.com.au

Copyright © Simon Johnson 1999

National Library of Australia Cataloguing-in-Publication data

Johnson, Simon.
Providore.

Includes Index.
ISBN 0 7336 0867 1

1. Food industry and trade - Australia. 2. Cookery. I. Title.
641.514

Produced by Brewster Publishers Pty Ltd
Designed by eskimo design
Printed in Australia by Griffin Press

CONTENTS

ACKNOWLEDGEMENTS

My thanks must go to the many chefs and friends whose recipes appear in the book:

Stephanie Alexander, Russell Armstrong, Maggie Beer, Tony Bilson, Andrew Blake, Laurent Boillon, Glen Bowman, Guillaume Brahimi, David Brown, Joan Campbell, Raymond Capaldi, Antonio Carluccio, Dany Chouet, Sherry Clewlow, Genevieve Copeland, Serge Dansereau, Greg Doyle, Matthew Fleming, Belinda Franks, Meera Freeman, Lucio Galletto, Bill Granger, Lorraine Godsmark, Joe Grilli, Alex Herbert, Prue Hill, Colin Holt, Ken Hom, Philip Johnson, Lew Kathreptis, Michael Klausen, Janni Kyritsis, Kylie Kwong, Michael Lambie, Kate Lamont, Ross Lusted, Rita Macali, Christine Manfield, Stefano Manfredi, Luke Mangan, Paul Merrony, Yvan Meunier, Michael Moore, Sean Moran, Anthony Musarra, Anders Ousback, Tony Papas, Neil Perry, Damien Pignolet, Dietmar Sawyere, Phillip Searle, Philippa Sibley-Cooke, Leigh Stone-Herbert, Jeremy Strode, Chris Taylor, Daryll Taylor, David Thompson, Liam Tomlin, John Wilson.

For their assistance with the text, thanks go to my good friends and colleagues Joan Campbell, Sue Fairlie Cuninghame, Leo Schofield, John Newton, Alison Stewart and John Wilson.

For her masterly design work on this book, my thanks to Natasha Hasemer, with special acknowledgement to Fred Rainey for his designs over the years. The publishers would also like to thank Kellie Hindmarch and Clare Forte.

This book includes the superb photographs taken for the Simon Johnson stores and catalogues over the years by Georgie Cole, Geoff Lung, Petrina Tinslay, William Meppem and Jean Paul Urizar. Additional photographs are from Oliver Strewe.

INTRODUCTION

During the Golden Age of foodyism in the late '60s, all of the '70s and the early part of the '80s, food, its preparation and consumption were bona fide leisure activities. This was the era of the food processor, of elaborate dinner parties, of cuisine nouvelle and cuisine minceur, of all manner of new products and new fads.

Then something strange happened. People began to run out of time. The new leisure we had been promised with the advent of high technology failed to materialise and most people found themselves working harder than they had ever done before. Gone suddenly were the days when a couple would spend two days chopping and stuffing and blending and basting to prepare dinner for four other couples. Food became something that had, of necessity, to be assembled faster.

There were two consequences of this revolution. The first was the proliferation of restaurants for those too busy and too whacked to prepare food for themselves. An irony, this: people working harder to earn more money so they could spend it having someone else do something they'd really like to be doing themselves. But the joy of preparing food oneself was not entirely obliterated, for the second consequence of the revolution was the emergence of the specialist food purveyor, of which Simon Johnson is the finest and most successful example we have here in Australia.

People no longer had to start from taws, dusting off the pasta making machine, preparing homemade tagliatelle, conjuring up a sublime sauce from scratch. Now it was done, at least in part, for them. A packet of splendid top quality pasta, preferably of some exotic form and name, a jar of pre-prepared sauce, a pot and some water were all that was needed to make an impressive meal. It was what the grander Englishman, accustomed to a live-in cook and maid, used to disparagingly describe as 'bought food', but it was far more delicious than most food that graced most English tables.

From Italy, Spain, France and from the best local suppliers, Johnson assembled a serious range of superb produce to make life easier on millennium man. And woman. He has also taught us that shopping for food can be a joy. Despite the closure of post offices, the replacement of friendly tellers with dysfunctional ATMs and Internet buying, our basic human need for contact with fellow human beings can still be satisfied by a visit to one of Simon's emporia cum salons, where coffee is dispensed to all comers and browsers are welcome.

What would we do without him? Work harder, I suspect. Drink coffee of lesser quality. Eat plastic pasta. Revert to over-salted anchovies in lieu of the exquisite ones we have become accustomed to. Johnson has changed our eating habits, brought a nice ease to the way we approach food. In the next generation hardly anyone will have heard of Beef Wellington, let alone have slaved to prepare it. Our palates have been born again. Long live the bloke who likes to describe himself clearly and accurately as the purveyor of quality foods.

LEO SCHOFIELD

Olives & Oils

'THE WHOLE mediterranean, THE SCULPTURE, THE PALMS, THE GOLD BEADS, THE BEARDED HEROES, THE WINE, THE IDEAS, THE SHIPS, THE MOONLIGHT, THE WINGED GORGONS, THE BRONZE MEN, THE PHILOSOPHERS — ALL OF IT SEEMS TO RISE IN THE SOUR, PUNGENT TASTE OF THESE BLACK olives BETWEEN THE TEETH. A TASTE older THAN MEAT, OLDER THAN WINE. A TASTE AS OLD AS COLD WATER.' PROSPERO'S CELL BY LAWRENCE DURRELL

THE ORIGINS OF THE OLIVE ARE LOST IN THE mists of time, BUT IT HAS BEEN IN CONTINUOUS CULTIVATION IN THE WESTERN WORLD FOR NEARLY 6000 YEARS. IT IS native TO THE MEDITERRANEAN, AND MORE THAN ANY OTHER FOOD IT EVOKES THE BRILLIANT CANVAS OF THAT AREA. MOST OLIVE OIL COMES FROM AROUND THE shores OF THE MEDITERRANEAN — SPAIN, FRANCE, ITALY, GREECE — WITH SPAIN, FOLLOWED BY ITALY, THE LEADING producers. BETWEEN THEM THEY PRODUCE MORE THAN HALF THE WORLD'S OLIVE OIL. OLIVES ARE ALSO GROWN NOW IN THE NEW WORLD; CALIFORNIA, SOUTH AMERICA AND AUSTRALIA. MOST PEOPLE IMAGINE THAT olive trees GROW BEST IN A DRY, DESERT-LIKE CLIMATE ON ROCKY ARID SOIL; HOWEVER, THEY GROW BEST IN A MILD MEDITERRANEAN climate WITH LONG, WARM SUMMERS AND COLD WINTERS.

SOIL THAT IS GOOD FOR GRAPE GROWING IS GENERALLY GOOD FOR OLIVES. ALTHOUGH PICTURE POSTCARDS OF MEDITERRANEAN COUNTRIES OFTEN SHOW OLIVE TREES GROWING ON rock-covered HILLSIDES, OLIVES ACTUALLY PREFER FERTILE SOIL, LIKE MOST FRUIT TREES. THE LONG-LIVING OLIVE TREE IS REASONABLY SLOW TO MATURE AND A THREE YEAR WAIT FOR THE FIRST FRUIT IS RECOGNISED AS NORMAL. IN THE ancient OLIVE GROVES, BEFORE IRRIGATION, THE TREES WERE PLANTED WIDE APART SO THEY DID NOT HAVE TO compete WITH ONE ANOTHER FOR WATER AND NUTRIENTS. THE TREES HAD MORE THAN ONE TRUNK AND SPREAD TO A GREAT SIZE. TODAY, olives ARE GROWN CLOSER TOGETHER WITH A SINGLE STRAIGHT TRUNK, AND THEY ARE PRUNED TO KEEP A LOW PROFILE THAT IS EASY TO HARVEST. LIKE THE difference BETWEEN CHARDONNAY GRAPES FOR WINE PRODUCTION AND SULTANA GRAPES FOR THE TABLE, OLIVE TREE varieties ARE SELECTED FOR THEIR SUITABILITY FOR THE TABLE OR FOR OLIVE OIL PRODUCTION. EVEN THEN THERE ARE MANY DIFFERENT VARIETIES AND, ALONG WITH THE CLIMATE AND terroir, THIS CAN CREATE A WIDE DIVERSITY OF FRUIT AND QUALITY.

OLIVE OIL

HARVEST

Picking the best time to harvest olives for oil is largely dependent upon what flavours are being sought. The longer the olives stay on the tree (i.e. the riper they are), the more oil they will produce, but the acidity also increases and the natural antioxidants, which help preserve the oil, and the flavour compounds start to diminish. It is a fine balance. Usually the estate-grown olives are picked while they are green, or just turning purple.

Olives are raked from the trees or mechanically harvested and pressed within a few hours of picking. The olives need to be pressed immediately to limit defects that can develop through poor storage resulting in fermentation of the fruit.

HOW OIL IS MADE

The challenge for the olive oil producer is to extract the oil from the olive while keeping the oil in optimum condition. Heat speeds up the degenerative processes and reduces the flavour and aroma.

Traditionally olives were crushed into a paste with huge granite mill-wheels and then pressed between fibre mats to release their oil. Today many of the steps to making olive oil have been enhanced by modern machinery, which is delivering greater quality control and finer oils. Smaller oilmakers still often use traditional techniques but apply modern methods and use the latest equipment.

Like winemaking, the use of modern technology has improved the purity of olive oil, reducing the risk of contaminants or taints.

COLONNA
(Italy)

A number of different olive varieties are grown on the Colonna estate in the Italian region of Molise. The olives are milled to a paste and then pressed to extract the oil from the olive juice. No heat is used and the result is an oil of exceptional purity.

However, the machinery is costly, so many small olive growers take their olives to an oil press. The olive grower can be sure that his olives, picked at their peak and carefully and quickly transported, will be crushed with perfectly clean equipment, allowing the flavours and quality to emerge.

The stainless steel hammers crush the olives and stones to a paste. This paste is transferred to a big stainless steel vat and rotated for about an hour, depending on the ripeness of the fruit, at a temperature controlled to stay below 28°C. From the vat it goes into a centrifuge decanter to separate the solids from the juice, then it goes into a separator where the oil and olive juice are separated. Many oils are filtered but the best are left to settle in tanks for a couple of months. The sediment settles on the bottom of the tank and the oil is skimmed from the top.

STYLES OF OLIVE OIL

Different countries and different regions within each country produce oils with quite different characteristics. The oils from Liguria and the Veneto in the north of Italy, for example, are known for being fruit driven, while central Tuscan and Umbrian oils are known for being green and leafy with a peppery taste, and southern Italian warmer climate oils are flavoursome and buttery. But there are buttery oils from the north and peppery ones from the south. Greek oils have their own styles and flavours, as do the Spanish oils. Each is influenced by the climate, the varieties, the season and the 'terroir', as well as the time between picking and processing and the method of processing. Oil from one estate and even one region can vary widely from year to year.

SIMON SAYS: USE THE BEST QUALITY OILS WHEN YOU CAN REALLY TASTE THEM: AS A DRESSING FOR PASTA WITH PARMESAN AND CHILLI OR DRIZZLED OVER FISH FRESH FROM THE BARBECUE.

AUSTRALIAN OLIVES

Olives have been grown in Australia since 1800, when a single olive tree was brought to Sydney by George Suttor, a market gardener and protege of Sir Joseph Banks. In 1844 the South Australian Company shipped 51 trees of five of the best oil-producing varietals from Marseilles. Oil produced from these trees, planted in gardens in Adelaide, received an honourable mention at the London Exhibition in 1851. In 1875 some 30,000 olive trees were planted near Adelaide. Slumps in the market for olive oil and a community that only used olive oil medicinally led to most of the olive groves being neglected.

A resurgence of interest came with the influx of Mediterranean immigrants whose food and lifestyles have influenced the rest of the community. Since the late 1980s olive oil has become a part of daily eating and Australia now imports millions of litres of olive oil every year. With a growing home market the production of olive oil in Australia now appears to be sustainable. As olives thrive in climates with warm summers and cool wet winters, many parts of Australia are suitable for planting. The expansion of the industry has begun, with one Queensland nursery alone selling a million trees—although they are predominantly table fruit varieties.

EXTRA VIRGIN OLIVE OIL

The division between virgin olive oils is usually the measurement of free oleic acid.

EXTRA VIRGIN OLIVE OIL has an acidity of less than 1 per cent and is made from the first pressing of olives.
VIRGIN OLIVE OIL has an acidity of less than 2 per cent.
ORDINARY VIRGIN OLIVE OIL has an acidity of less than 3.3 per cent.
LIGHT OLIVE OIL is refined oil with just a little extra virgin oil added so that it has a light clear colour. It contains the same amount of kilojoules as any olive oil — the 'light' label refers to its mild flavour, not its fat levels.

The International Olive Oil Council's definition of virgin olive oils has three components:

The oils must be extracted from sound olives by the mechanical processes of milling, pressing and centrifuging. Chemical and high heat extraction is not allowed.

The oils must pass a number of tests for detecting additives such as vegetable oils.

The oil must pass a sensory evaluation from a tasting panel.

The virgin olive oils are labelled according to acidity—low acidity is a characteristic of extra virgin oil — but labelling can be a trap. Although first-pressed high quality olives yield oil of low acidity, inferior refined oils can be treated with an alkaline solution to lower oleic acidity and achieve an extra virgin label. This is why the International Olive Oil Council has brought in sensory evaluation.

THE INTERNATIONAL OLIVE OIL COUNCIL

The International Olive Oil Council is an international organisation that has established sensory evaluation panels composed of accredited olive oil tasting judges. Fifteen Australians have been trained by the Australian Olive Oil Association to become accredited judges, Simon Johnson among them. Their job is not to nominate one oil as being better than another, but to judge oils according to their positive attributes and defects and to categorise them into extra virgin, virgin, refined and lampante. In an official oil tasting, the appearance of the oil does not count and blue glasses are used to conceal the oil. The pursuit of excellence is the primary focus. This evaluation by trained tasters is a much better standard to use when buying olive oil than the acidity rating, which can be chemically adulterated. The Council is promoting a system where all refined olive oils would be

required to be evaluated. In this way, only traditionally made extra virgin olive oils would qualify to be labelled extra virgin.

TASTIN OLIVE OIL

Oil experts have almost as broad a tasting vocabulary as wine experts, using terms such as almond, spice, grass, hay, metallic, fruity and peppery to describe different flavours. And they go about tasting in much the same way — pouring a little of each oil into glasses and comparing the smell, then inhaling before sipping a little, aspirating while holding it in the mouth, then spitting it out. Unlike wine tasters, who may taste up to 20 wines in a session, oil experts rarely taste more than six.

Try tasting as many different styles from different regions as possible, but not all at once — two or three at a time is enough. Rub some into the palms of your hands and smell the aroma, or pour some into a glass and warm the glass in your cupped hands then take a deep sniff to get an impression. Dip bread into each oil and taste it, or take a sip and swill a little around the mouth. Swallow it or spit it out; you will soon find your favourites.

Try a small dish of extra virgin olive oil and some crusty bread to dip into it at the table instead of bread with butter.

SIMON SAYS: THE BEST WAY TO DECIDE UPON AN OLIVE OIL IS TO TASTE IT. A GOOD EXTRA VIRGIN OLIVE OIL HAS A BALANCE OF THREE POSITIVE ATTRIBUTES:

FRUIT: THERE SHOULD BE AN OBVIOUS OLIVE FLAVOUR.

BITTERNESS: NOT TOO MUCH, BUT ENOUGH TO REDUCE THE OIL'S CLOYING CHARACTER.

PUNGENCY: A SPICY PEPPERY TASTE IS ALWAYS PRESENT WHEN LESS THAN RIPE FRUIT IS USED. YOU TEND TO NOTICE IT AS AN AFTERTASTE.

STORING OLIVE OIL

No matter how attractive some olive oil bottles are, your oil will become rancid if you store it on a sunny shelf. Keep oil in a cool dark place; not the refrigerator where it will solidify, and never near the stove. Exposure to air brings on oxidation, which turns oil rancid, and heat speeds up the degenerative processes, reducing the flavour and aroma. Olive oil can usually be stored for up to two years after opening but its flavour will decline the longer you keep it — unlike wine, olive oils do not improve with age. Some very young oils will lose their sharp taste and become more mellow in the first few months, but as a general rule, when you buy your oil it is as good as it gets.

PRIMO ESTATE
(Virginia, South Australia)

Joe Grilli of Primo Estate makes olive oil from olives gathered from South Australia's backyards. Some of the trees are majestic, dating back to the 1850s, but most are 40 to 50 years old and were planted by migrants who arrived in Australia in the 1950s and 1960s. Joe also has 500 of his own trees planted and he buys olives from small groves. The fruit is picked at the half-green/half-purple stage in March, April and May, and is processed using a blend of traditional and modern methods. The oil is usually stored for eight weeks to allow it to settle before bottling.

SIMON SAYS: WITHOUT JOE GRILLI THE OLIVE OIL INDUSTRY IN AUSTRALIA WOULD NOT HAVE DEVELOPED AS QUICKLY AS IT HAS. HIS ANNUAL OUTPUT IS SMALL, BUT HIS EXPERIENCE AND SKILL AS A WINEMAKER HAS ENABLED HIM TO PRODUCE FINE TABLE OIL THAT BALANCES THE VARIOUS NUANCES OF THIS 'PATCHWORK' OF RAW MATERIALS. HE IS A MASTER BLENDER.

NOVELLO MOSTO

This is the name for the new season's oil—it is unfiltered and very cloudy but it has a fresh herbaceous flavour. Joe Grilli of Primo Estate produces a first run extra virgin oil that is made from the first of the season's olives and released in April .

AFFIORATO

Affiorato (flower of the oil) literally means 'to emerge' and that's how the Umbrian Mancianti oil is made. The hand-picked olives are stone-milled for longer than is usual, and the oil that emerges from the paste after milling but before pressing is skimmed off. This is *affiorato*, and it represents only 5 per cent of the total production of the Mancianti label.

SIMON SAYS: UMBRIA IS ONE OF THE FAMOUS OLIVE OIL PRODUCING REGIONS OF ITALY AND PRODUCES SOME OF THE WORLD'S GREAT OLIVE OILS.

SALSA VERDE

Kate Lamont | Lamont's Wine & Food

Makes 1 1/2 cups

1 clove garlic, peeled and chopped
2 anchovy fillets
1 tablespoon salted capers, well rinsed
1/2 cup flat leaf parsley, chopped
1 bunch chives, chopped
1 stalk rosemary, chopped
50 ml red wine vinegar
freshly ground pepper
200 ml olive oil

Place the garlic, anchovies, capers, herbs and red wine vinegar in a food processor. Season with pepper and turn on the processor. Slowly drizzle in the oil with the processor running. Pour a little salsa verde over mushroom risotto, grilled fish or barbecued lamb.

POLLO BOLLITO CON PATE DI BASILICO

Joe Grilli | Primo Estate

Serves 4

2 chicken breast fillets
1 onion
1/2 carrot
1 stick celery (including leaves)
1/2 bay leaf
1 clove
1/2 teaspoon salt
salt and freshly ground black pepper
Joseph extra virgin olive oil
Forum cabernet sauvignon vinegar
Pâté di basilico (see page 21)
Empeltre olives
ripe tomatoes

Place the chicken, onion, carrot, celery, bay leaf and clove in a saucepan. Cover with water and add the salt. Bring gently to the boil, then simmer for about 20 minutes or until the chicken is cooked. Remove the chicken, strain the stock and use for soup.

Slice the chicken, sprinkle with the salt and the pepper then drizzle with the extra virgin olive oil and vinegar. Serve with pâté di basilico and black olives or slices of ripe tomatoes.

PATE DI BASILICO

Joe Grilli | Primo Estate

Makes about 2 cups

2 tablespoons pine nuts

1 bunch fresh basil, torn

1 clove garlic, crushed

salt and freshly ground black pepper

10 sun-dried tomatoes

2 tablespoons fresh breadcrumbs

1/4 cup Joseph extra virgin olive oil

2 tablespoons grated parmigiano reggiano cheese

Toast the pine nuts by placing them in a dry frying pan and cooking over a high heat, shaking the pan frequently, until golden. Be careful that they do not burn.

Place the basil leaves, pine nuts, garlic, salt, pepper, sun-dried tomatoes and breadcrumbs in a food processor and process the mixture until smooth. With the processor still running, add the oil in a thin steady stream to form a thick paste. Turn the mixture into a bowl, add the parmigiano and mix until combined.

LAUDEMIO
(Tuscany, Italy)

Throughout Italy there are many consortiums or co-operatives of growers who together market their olive oils under the one label. Laudemio is an example of this. It is a consortium of more than 30 independent estates from the hills of central Tuscany between Florence and Sienna. The name of the individual estate from which the oil comes is printed on the Laudemio label. The members of the consortium, known as *gli olivanti*, are required to follow certain guidelines: the olives must be hand picked, they must be cold pressed and very little time must elapse between harvesting and pressing.

RAVIDA
(Sicily, Italy)

Until Ravida started winning prizes for its extra virgin olive oil, Sicily was not a renowned oil-producing region. But in 1993 they won a national competition, beating 70 other oils from around Italy, and in 1996 Ravida won two gold awards for their extra virgin olive oil.

Ravida oil is made from 50 per cent Biancolilla olives, light green in colour, which give the oil its aroma and delicacy; 45 per cent Cerasuola olives, which provide the full-bodied smoothness and five per cent Nocellara del Belice olives, an eating olive that gives the oil a fruitiness.

Harvesting begins in the first week of November when the Cerasuola olives turn from green to violet and the other two varieties are still green. The olives are picked by hand with the help of vibrating combs that cause the olives to fall into nets placed under each tree. Processing starts within eight hours of picking and the oil is left unfiltered.

SPAGHETTI, PEPPERONCINI, REGGIANO

Michael Moore

Serves 2

2 stuffed pepperoncini
180g spaghetti
60 ml extra virgin olive oil
juice of 1 lemon
90g rocket leaves
sea salt and freshly ground pepper
90g parmigiano reggiano cheese, shaved

Roughly chop the pepperoncini, retaining the stuffing and a little of the oil.

Cook the spaghetti al dente. Drain and refresh with cold water if you would prefer a cold dish; otherwise leave hot.

In a bowl mix the spaghetti with the chopped pepperoncini. Dress with the olive oil and lemon juice, mix in the rocket leaves and season with salt and pepper.

Serve with cheese shavings.

MARINADE OF RAW TUNA WITH DILL AND CUCUMBER

Paul Merrony | Merronys

Serves 4

150 ml homemade mayonnaise (see below)
20g French mustard
80 ml cream
1 tablespoon chives, chopped
1 small bunch dill, finely chopped
1/2 small cucumber, finely sliced
4 x 60g very fine escalopes of tuna, flattened slightly with a heavy knife
drained feta cheese, cut in 1 cm dice

Mix together the mayonnaise, French mustard and cream. When well mixed, add the chives and dill and allow to stand for the flavours to infuse.

Bring a pot of salted water to the boil and toss in the cucumber slices. When they have turned an appealing translucent green, remove them from the boiling water and refresh in iced water.

Place the tuna slices onto four cold plates and sprinkle liberally with the feta cheese. Drizzle some of the mayonnaise over the tuna and feta and then lay the blanched cucumber slices over the top. Drizzle over the sauce once again and serve. This recipe is delicious with crusty, chunky toast.

HOMEMADE MAYONNAISE

Paul Merrony | Merronys

Makes about 2 cups

1 egg yolk
squeeze of lemon
salt and freshly ground pepper
250 ml olive oil

To make the mayonnaise: Blend the egg yolk, lemon juice, salt and pepper in a blender and with the processor still running gradually add the olive oil. Refrigerate the mayonnaise until it is required.

OLIVES

There are many types of olive suitable for eating, with a wide range of sizes and flavours. Their taste depends not only on their variety and at what stage of ripeness they were picked, but also on how they have been processed.

The traditional method of removing olives' bitterness is by soaking them in pure water, changing the water every day, for about 15 days. The olives are then put into a brine for several months. Black olives are cured for a shorter time than green olives.

Serve olives, black or green, stuffed or plain, with drinks before dinner or as part of an antipasto or meze platter.

If you have access to a tree with good quality eating olives there is a simple way to preserve them at home. Pick the riper olives when they are turning black or are already black (they will be at different stages). Place a layer of salt in the bottom of a hessian bag and sprinkle in a layer of olives. Cover the olives with more salt and continue layering until all the olives are well covered in salt. Tie the top of the bag and hang it in an airy dry spot. Every few days give the olives a mix by squeezing and pushing the bag so the olives move around and remain covered in salt. Leave the bag for at least a month. The olives are cured when they no longer taste bitter. Rinse the salt from the olives and pack them into jars. Cover the olives with olive oil. Flavourings such as sprigs of thyme or chillies can be added to the jars. Seal and store in a cool dark place.

MANZANILLA from Andalusia in Spain, a small, pale green fine-textured olive, is the most delicate and smooth-tasting of all Spanish olives. A manzanilla is the correct olive to serve in a martini. They are especially delicious stuffed with aromatic dried anchovies.

GORDAL, which is also called a queen olive or sevillano olive, is large, deep green and fleshy. It is considered by many to be Spain's finest olive.

EMPELTRE, a black olive from southern Spain, is regarded as Spain's answer to the kalamata olive.

ARBEQUIÑA, from Catalana in northern Spain, is small and an unusual brown-green colour. This is one of the few table varieties that also makes very good extra virgin olive oil.

BELLA CERIGNOLA olives are big and green, fresh tasting and crunchy in texture.

TAGGIASCHE olives from Liguria in Italy are picked when they are greeny purple. They are small and are the same variety as the French niçoise olives.

BRUSCHETTA D'ESTATE

Joe Grilli | Primo Estate

Serves 4–6

3 ripe tomatoes

2 Lebanese cucumbers

1/2 Spanish onion

100g of your favourite young cheese (e.g. feta or bocconcini)

20 kalamata olives or anchovy stuffed olives, sliced

salt and freshly ground pepper

Joseph extra virgin olive oil

sour dough bread

1 clove garlic

Remove the seeds from the tomatoes and cucumbers. Finely dice the
tomatoes, cucumbers and onion and place in a serving bowl with the
crumbled or sliced cheese and olives. Add salt and freshly ground
pepper to taste. Add enough oil to coat all the ingredients when
mixed, then let stand for at least 30 minutes. Serve on sourdough
bread that has been grilled and lightly rubbed with garlic.

PIZZA OF ROASTED PUMPKIN WITH FETA AND OLIVES

Glen Bowman | The Centennial Hotel

Serves 2–4

Pizza dough (see page 43)

Pizza sauce:
1/2 leek, washed and finely sliced
1 small brown onion, peeled and finely chopped
2 cloves garlic, peeled and minced
olive oil
375g can Italian peeled tomatoes, chopped
salt and freshly ground pepper
1/2 teaspoon sugar
1 bunch basil, leaves chopped
1 bunch parsley, leaves chopped

Topping:
1 butternut pumpkin, peeled and chopped
1 tablespoon rosemary, chopped
2 tablespoons parmesan, grated
2 tablespoons mozzarella, grated
1 cup herbs: parsley, basil, sage, marjoram, oregano, chopped
50g Meredith feta cheese, chopped
10 olives, pitted
salt and freshly ground pepper

TO MAKE THE PIZZA SAUCE: In a heavy-based saucepan over medium heat sauté the leek, onion and garlic in olive oil until translucent. Add the tomatoes and simmer for 20 minutes. Season to taste with salt, pepper and sugar. Allow to cool and add the herbs.

TO MAKE THE TOPPING: Roast the pumpkin with some chopped rosemary in a 200°C oven until golden brown. Allow to cool.

TO MAKE THE PIZZA: Roll the pizza dough out on a lightly floured surface. Spread the pizza sauce on the base. Sprinkle with some of the grated parmesan, mozzarella and the herb mixture. Arrange the pumpkin, feta and olives on top. Sprinkle with more parmesan, mozzarella and herbs. Season with salt and pepper.

Bake in a preheated oven at 220°C for approximately 15 minutes or until the base is crisp.

OLIVE PASTES AND TAPENADES

Many olive oil producers have made tapenades and olive pastes for family and friends for years, and now they're starting to offer them to the world. These tapenades, made from the finest olives, are crushed and blended with extra virgin olive oil.

Try tapenade stirred into hot pasta or soup, or spread on foccacia. Or make sophisticated toast soldiers for your boiled egg by spreading them thinly with tapenade.

SIMON SAYS: THE TAPENADES TO BUY ARE THOSE MADE BY THE OLIVE OIL PRODUCERS WHO MAKE THEM IN SEASON WITH THEIR BEST OLIVES AND THEIR BEST EXTRA VIRGIN OIL. MARIA POSSENTI OF UMBRIA WHO MAKES A RANGE OF PATES FROM BOTH BLACK AND GREEN OLIVES, BLENDED WITH THEIR OWN EXTRA VIRGIN OLIVE OIL, AND THE SOMMARIVA ESTATE OF LIGURIA AND SALVAGNO IN VENETO PRODUCE EXCELLENT OLIVE PASTE MADE FROM THE OLIVES AND OIL FROM THEIR OWN GROVES.

HOMEMADE TAPENADE

Remove the stones from 250g of black olives. Place the olives in a food processor with 2 teaspoons capers, 4 anchovy fillets, 1 peeled and crushed garlic clove, chopped parsley, freshly ground black pepper and 1 teaspoon of cognac. Process to a rough purée. If the tapenade is too thick, pour some extra virgin olive oil into the processor and process until the mixture is the right consistency. To store, pour over 1 ml of extra virgin olive oil, cover and refrigerate. The tapenade should keep for several weeks.

FLAVOURED OILS

Flavoured oils have their very own place in the pantry; these are mostly infused oils and oils that have a flavouring essence added. These oils have distinctive flavours such as lemon pepper, chilli, garlic, truffle and black pepper, and can be used in vinaigrettes, marinades, or drizzled over salads, foccacia or pasta. They should not be confused with citrus and nut oils, which are made by pressing out the oils contained in fruit zests or nut kernels.

You can make your own flavoured oils by infusing the flavours of fresh herbs, chillies or garlic in olive oil. Some herbs make wonderfully decorative flavoured oils—rosemary, for instance, particularly if you can find some sprigs in flower. Flavoured oils look so attractive it's tempting to put them out on display, but they should be stored the same way as any other oil — in a cool, dark place.

CHILLI OIL

Sean Moran | Panaroma

Makes 1 1/2 litres

500g long red chillies, split and de-seeded
1 litre olive oil
1/2 head garlic, peeled

Place the chillies into a heavy-based pan with the oil and garlic. Cook gently over a moderate heat until the moisture has evaporated— it will appear golden and smell nutty. Remove from the heat to cool. Strain the pulp from the oil and purée to a smooth paste. Combine with the oil and store in a sealed glass jar in a cool dark place.

SHORTCUT

Michael Klausen | Bayswater Brasserie

Mix black pepper oil with balsamic vinegar and serve over barbecued octopus on a salad of rocket and oven-dried tomatoes.

SNAPPER PIES

Yvan Meunier | Boathouse

Makes 4 large pies, serves 8

8 medium onions, peeled and sliced
olive oil
400 ml fish stock
800 ml cream
2 medium onions, diced
salt and freshly ground pepper
1 kg puff pastry
1 kg pink snapper fillets
4 dessertspoons white truffle oil
1 egg, lightly beaten with a little water

Sauté the sliced onions with 1 tablespoon of olive oil. Add the fish stock. Reduce until the onions take on a very light brown colour. Add the cream. Reduce by half or until a thick creamy consistency is reached. Cool and blend in a processor until smooth.

In a separate pan sauté the diced onions in a little olive oil until soft. Combine with the cream sauce and season to taste with salt and pepper.

Roll the puff pastry to 5 mm thick and cut it into ovals to cover four ramekins (17.5 x 12.5 x 5 cm), making each 3 cm wider than the ramekin. Into each ramekin spoon about 2 tablespoons of the sauce. Lay the snapper on top of the sauce, top with another tablespoon of the sauce and a dessertspoon of truffle oil. Cover with a pastry lid and press down the sides. Glaze with egg wash. Cook for 25 minutes in a preheated 260°C oven. Rest for 8 minutes before serving.

CITRUS OILS

Oils made from citrus fruits (orange, lemon and lime) are extreme-ly pungent and should be used sparingly. These are the natural oils cold pressed from the zest of the fruit — the bottled essence has the aroma of a citrus orchard. They have a powerfully intense flavour without the fruit's acid, and can be used in place of peel or zest — a useful way of adding citrus flavour without the bulk of juice or peel.

SIMON SAYS: AS IT TAKES ABOUT 600 LIMES TO MAKE ONE BOTTLE OF LIME OIL, YOU ONLY NEED A DROP OR TWO TO GIVE A POWERFUL LIME FLAVOUR.

PANNACOTTA WITH VANILLA AND ORANGE

Anthony Musarra | Lucciola
Serves 6

125 ml milk
375 ml cream
75g sugar
1 vanilla bean, scraped
1 cinnamon stick, broken
1 piece orange zest
1 1/2 leaves gelatine, softened in cold water for 4 minutes
1/2 teaspoon orange oil

Gently heat the milk, cream and sugar with the vanilla bean, cinnamon and orange zest. Bring slowly to the boil, stirring until the sugar dissolves. Remove from the heat and add the gelatine and orange oil, stir until the gelatine has dissolved. Cool, strain, pour into 1/2 cup capacity moulds and refrigerate overnight. To serve: dip the moulds in hot water, turn out and serve with fresh figs or berries and a little orange syrup.

NUT OILS

Nut oils are made by first crushing the nuts and pounding them until they reach peanut butter consistency. The paste is gently toasted, which brings out the natural flavour, and then it is spread in layers in a mould and huge pressure is exerted. Twenty-five kilograms of nuts are needed to yield about thirteen litres of oil. The oil is left to settle in vats for a week so the sediment sinks to the bottom before the oil is bottled. These oils are delicate and oxidise easily if exposed to the air, so keep sealed and store in a cool dark place.

SIMON SAYS: THESE ARE NOTHING LIKE THE NUT OILS THAT WERE OVER-USED IN THE 1970S: THE FLAVOUR IS STRONG AND INTENSE AND THE OILS SHOULD BE USED SPARINGLY. THEY ARE DELICIOUS OVER GREEN BEANS OR WITH DUCK AND GAME.

LOAVES

SHORTCUTS

Mix almond oil with a little lemon juice and coat lightly steamed asparagus. Drizzle walnut oil over sliced roasted beetroot for a delicious winter salad. Make a vinaigrette of walnut oil and wine vinegar and use it on a salad of shredded duck confit and winter greens.

WATERCRESS AND WITLOF SALAD, WITH PEARL BARLEY AND BLUE CHEESE AND WALNUT DRESSING

Luke Mangan | Salt
Serves 4

200g pearl barley
sea salt
150 ml extra virgin olive oil
100 ml pure cream
chives, finely chopped
freshly ground pepper
1 medium sized bunch watercress
1 large head witlof
50 ml sherry vinegar
100 ml walnut oil
200g Milawa Oxley Blue cheese, at room temperature
1 red capsicum, peeled and cut into diamond shapes

Soak the pearl barley in water for 24 hours. Drain and place in a saucepan. Cover with cold water and a pinch of sea salt and cook for about one hour or until tender. Drain well and let cool. Once cool, place in a food processor and blend, adding a little of the olive oil and the cream. Mix well, add the chives and season to taste with the pepper. Set aside.

Pick over the watercress, leaving a little of the stem on. Separate the witlof spears and gently break or cut in half. Mix together. Combine the sherry vinegar and walnut oil and drizzle over the watercress and witlof; mix well. Heap some of the pearl barley mixture in the centre of each plate. Place watercress and witlof on top, getting as much height as possible. Crumble the blue cheese over the salad. Scatter the capsicum diamonds over the plate. Drizzle with the remaining olive oil.

YOU CAN MAKE A *loaf* OF BREAD WITH NOTHING MORE THAN FLOUR, WATER, SOME YEAST AND TIME. GIVEN ENOUGH TIME, YOU CAN EVEN DISPENSE WITH THE YEAST AND USE THE WILD YEASTS IN THE AIR. THIS WAS HOW THE *early leavens* WERE MADE: A MIXTURE OF GROUND MEAL AND WATER WAS LEFT IN THE WARMTH OF THE SUN AND THE RESULT WAS RISEN *dough* — SOFT AND AIRY AND READY TO BAKE. WHEN BREAD MAKING BECAME A COMMERCIAL PROCESS IT FREED THE *home cook* FROM THE NEED TO BAKE BREAD DAILY, BUT WE WENT BACKWARDS IN TERMS OF TASTE, TEXTURE AND VARIETY. FORTUNATELY, CONSUMER PRESSURE WAS NOT TO BE DENIED. OVER THE PAST FEW YEARS THERE HAVE BEEN BIG CHANGES IN BREAD. AS AN ALTERNATIVE TO THE UBIQUITOUS SLICED LOAF WE CAN BUY WOOD-FIRED HARD-CRUSTED *italian* BREAD, GENUINE CRISP-CRUSTED FRENCH BREAD AND, BEST OF ALL, HEAVY-CRUSTED *sourdough* BREAD. THE ROLE OF THE BAKER IS AGAIN RISING IN APPRECIATION OF THE ART OF BREADMAKING.

BREADMAKING

Time is really the key to successful breadmaking. Just as wine ages and cheese ripens, yeast must have the time to do its work in the dough. Yeast not only aerates the dough, it enhances the flavour and texture. While the yeast is at work it allows the glutens in the flour to go through a slow ripening process. The important principle behind yeast cooking is to allow the time for slow yeast development so as to allow the ripening process to take place. This is why the traditional process is long and slow with several risings.

Up until the 1800s, bread was made using a yeast starter from the previous day's dough. It was difficult to use and sometimes unreliable in its outcomes. The 1870s brought the sort of yeast we use today and the reliable bread styles and flavours. The flours used for most good breads are high in gluten strength and this is where the term 'strong' flour has come from. Flour used for bread is also sometimes called 'bakers' flour.

The modern baker's oven has a very hot firebrick floor and a steam injection system which adds humidity to the oven. The steam helps to give extra volume to the dough and also helps to brown the crust. The high heat of the brick floor gives the oven an even heat and the bread a firm crust on the base.

THE FOLLOWING ARE SOME OF THE MOST COMMON TYPES OF BREAD.

WHITE: Made from white flour milled from wheat, white bread comes in a great variety of shapes, from ordinary square loaves to French baguettes. Seeds, such as poppy or sesame, are often used as toppings on white bread rolls.

WHOLEMEAL, WHOLEGRAIN OR WHEATMEAL: Made from at least 90 per cent flour milled from the whole grain, usually wheat. Up to 10 per cent white flour may be used.

MIXED GRAIN: Made from white and/or wholemeal flour with kibbled grains, usually rye and/or wheat, added. Vogel bread was the prototype.

RYE: Must contain at least 30 per cent rye flour, but darker varieties, such as pumpernickel, contain much more and have a strong flavour suited to strongly flavoured foods, such as smoked fish and cheese. A staple in Germany, Russia and Scandinavian countries, rye bread keeps well.

SOURDOUGH: The ancient Egyptians discovered that a flour and water dough exposed to airborne yeast spores would ferment and produce a leavened bread. A fresh batch could be 'started' by using some of the dough from the previous batch. It was a simple but slow method — taking days rather than hours — to leaven bread. European settlers took the tradition to America, and Californian goldminers introduced it to Australia during the 1850s goldrush.

DAMPER: A bread made with self-raising flour, although some commercial dampers are yeast-leavened and almost identical to ordinary white bread. Traditional damper originated in colonial days and was on the daily menu for drovers and other bushmen who baked it in the hot ashes of their camp fires.

FOCACCIA: Made from a simple white flour dough similar to pizza, it comes in a variety of thicknesses and shapes in Italy, where it originated. In Australia it is usually about 3 cm thick and rectangular.

FLAT BREADS: These breads are common throughout the Middle

SOURDOUGH BREAD

A good sourdough bread is characterised by a thick crust and a delicious, slightly tangy flavour. Sourdough breads are made with a sourdough starter — usually flour, water and sugar (sometimes the sugar is replaced by fruit pulp). It is left to ferment for about three days in a warm place and is then used as a leavener in the bread. In some sourdough breads a little yeast is used as well, but much less than is used in ordinary yeast-leavened bread. Sourdough bread has excellent keeping qualities. And the starter, if stored in the right conditions and added to regularly, can last for years. Sourdough is good with cheese or brushed with oil and grilled for bruschetta.

East and India and can be leavened, such as Turkish, or unleavened, such as matzo. Other varieties include mountain bread, pita, lavash, naan, paratha and chapatti.

TO MAKE SOURDOUGH BREAD

Tony Papas | Bayswater Brasserie

Tony Papas makes sourdough bread starter using organically grown green grapes which are crushed then squeezed through a muslin cloth. To this is added an equal quantity of unbleached flour, then the mixture is covered and left to stand in a warm place for about three days. The starter has to be fed with a mixture of flour and water daily—at the very least every two days—or it will die.

To make a sourdough loaf the starter is combined with water, flour and salt, then kneaded. It is put in a warm place to double in size for about 4–5 hours, then left to rest for 20 minutes. The dough is then knocked back, shaped into a ball, left to prove for another hour and then refrigerated overnight. The following day it is brought back to room temperature and baked in a 250°C preheated oven turned down to 210°C as soon as the bread goes in. It cooks for about 45 minutes. Rye flour and malt are added to make a rye sourdough loaf.

SHORTCUT

Panzanella

Cut the top off a loaf of sourdough bread and scoop out and discard some of the soft bread. Heat the loaf in a moderate oven for 10 minutes, sprinkle the insides liberally with extra virgin olive oil and fill it with a mixture of chopped tomato, red onion, torn basil and rocket leaves, chunks of marinated feta and pitted olives. To eat it you tear off chunks of warm bread and use it to scoop up some of the filling.

SHORTCUT

Croutons

Cut good quality Italian bread into 2 cm squares and place in a roasting pan with a generous splash of olive oil. Toss well so that the bread is coated with oil. Bake in a preheated oven at 180°C for 10–15 minutes or until golden. Toss and drain on kitchen paper.

GRISSINI (LITTLE BREADSTICKS)

Stephanie Alexander

olive oil
finely chopped garlic
fennel seeds
salt
freshly ground black pepper

Dough:
250g unbleached flour
1 teaspoon salt
2 teaspoons dried yeast
1 teaspoon honey
1 tablespoon olive oil
1/2 cup water

TO MAKE THE DOUGH: Combine all the ingredients and knead well until smooth. Put the dough into a lightly greased bowl, then cover with a tea towel and allow to stand in a draught-free spot until the dough has doubled in size, about one hour. Knock back gently. Allow the dough to double in size again, about 30 minutes.

Meanwhile, preheat the oven to 180°C. Break off small pieces of dough the size of a walnut and roll each into a thin sausage about 25 cm long. Pour olive oil into a shallow tray, then add some garlic, fennel seeds, salt and pepper and drag each grissini through this mixture. Space well apart on a floured baking tray and bake without delay for 15 minutes until browned and crisp.

BRIOCHE

These are the buttery, light breads of France usually served with coffee for breakfast. The difference between brioche and bread is that eggs are used rather than water or milk and a large proportion of butter is used.

BRIOCHE
Serves 4

200 ml milk
60g fresh yeast
6 egg yolks
500g plain flour
150g unsalted butter

Heat the milk until just warm and dissolve the yeast in it. Add the yolks and mix together. Sift the flour into a bowl and add the yeast and egg mixture while beating slowly. Now add the butter in 50g pieces. Mix until smooth. Transfer to a large bowl, cover and put in a warm place until the dough doubles in size.

Knead the dough on a floured board until it is smooth. Shape the dough into eight large balls and eight small balls. Place the large balls in eight individual, lightly buttered brioche or fluted moulds and place the smaller balls on top. Cover lightly and let stand in a warm place until they have doubled in size. Bake in a preheated oven at 200°C for 20–25 minutes.

PANETTONE

Panettone is an Italian version of brioche — it is made using the same basic ingredients of milk, flour, yeast, eggs and butter. However the shapes, flavourings such as dried fruit or chocolate, and the amount of sweetness varies widely from region to region.

PETER STAFFORD'S BREAD AND BUTTER PUDDING

Joan Campbell

Serves 6

1/2 cup sultanas
1 panettone
soft butter
5 eggs
4 tablespoons sugar
2/3 cup cream
2 cups milk
soft butter for the top of the pudding
grated nutmeg
cream

Soak the sultanas in hot water for a few minutes to plump them up, then drain well and set aside. Cut the panettone into enough thin slices to make two layers in your pudding dish. Butter one side of the panettone slices.

Scatter half of the sultanas in the pudding dish then cover with a layer of panettone, buttered side down.

Beat the eggs with the sugar and add the cream and milk. Pour half the custard mix into the pudding dish and cover with another layer of panettone, buttered side up. Scatter over the remaining sultanas and pour in the remaining custard mix. Dot with butter and dust with nutmeg.

Place the dish in a tin of hot water, making sure the water comes halfway up the sides of the dish. Bake on the centre shelf of a 180°C preheated oven for one hour. Serve with fresh cream.

CROISSANTS

The traditional croissant is made from a risen yeast, milk and flour dough. It is flattened, folded and rolled with many additions of butter, as if making puff pastry.

PIZZA

The traditional pizza is never baked in a pan but upon the hot brick surface of a baker's style oven. This gives it a crisp, thin crust. Pizza dough goes through a single, fairly rapid rising. The dough should be elastic with a faintly sour yeasty taste. Pizza can be cooked in 10 minutes on the hot firebricks of the baker's oven. In the home oven it will take longer.

SIMON SAYS: FOR THE BEST RESULT AT HOME PUT ONE OR TWO LARGE UNGLAZED TERRACOTTA TILES IN YOUR OVEN TO COOK YOUR PIZZA ON.

PIZZA DOUGH
Makes 1 large pizza

200g plain flour
1 teaspoon salt
1 tablespoon olive oil
8g sachet dried yeast
8 tablespoons warm water

Sift the flour into a bowl and make a shallow well in the centre. Dissolve the yeast in the warm water.

Put the salt, dissolved yeast and olive oil into the well and combine the flour with the other ingredients. Form into a ball with your hands. Knead the mixture for seven minutes.

If using a food processor, place the dry ingredients into the bowl, then slowly add the dissolved yeast and the olive oil while the processor is running. Process until a ball is formed. Remove the dough and knead it for about five minutes.

Put the dough in a lightly floured bowl and cover with a damp tea towel. Place the bowl in a warm place and leave for up to three hours until the dough has doubled in volume.

FISHES

WILD FISH, LIKE THE wilderness, ARE A LIMITED RESOURCE THAT MUST

BE PROTECTED. THE GROWTH IN FARMED FISH AND METHODS OF PRESERVING FISH

HAVE ALLOWED PEOPLE ALL AROUND THE WORLD TO EXPERIENCE THE taste OF

SOME OF THE MOST SOUGHT AFTER freshwater AND SALTWATER FISH

WHICH CAN NO LONGER BE HARVESTED IN GREAT QUANTITIES IN THE WILD; THESE

INCLUDE salmon, OYSTERS AND CAVIAR. SMOKING, DRYING AND SALTING

WERE METHODS OF PRESERVING SEAFOOD LONG BEFORE COMMERCIAL

PROCESSING WAS INTRODUCED — AND SMOKING IS ONE OF THE oldest

METHODS OF FOOD PRESERVATION. ORIGINALLY, THESE TECHNIQUES SPRANG

FROM necessity, BUT NOW FOOD IS SMOKED MAINLY BECAUSE OF THE

RESULTING DISTINCTIVE FLAVOURS.

SALMON

Wild salmon is still commercially fished in western Canada and Scotland; however, the scarcity of fish has led to limits being put in place to protect fish stocks. Wild salmon take anywhere from three to five years to complete their life cycle. They are an anadromous fish, meaning they have a freshwater phase and a marine phase. They begin as a pea-sized egg in a river, where they hatch and then migrate to the sea as smolts. Under natural conditions, smoltification takes place in the spring as water temperature and day length increase.

Salmon spend two to four years in salt water, growing rapidly, until they reach maturity and return to the rivers to spawn and complete their life cycle. Farm raised fish follow the same natural cycle as wild salmon but in a farm environment.

SIMON SAYS: THINLY SLICE RAW SALMON AND ARRANGE IN A SINGLE LAYER ON A SERVING PLATE. DRIZZLE WITH OLIVE OIL AND SPRINKLE WITH FRESHLY GROUND MIXED PEPPERCORNS AND FINELY GRATED LEMON ZEST. JUST BEFORE SERVING DRIZZLE WITH LEMON JUICE.

SMOKED SALMON

The best salmon is cold smoked after it has been dry cured with sea salt for 8 to 16 hours. Cold smoking (in which the temperature never exceeds 30°C) means that the salmon is smoked without being cooked. The fish slowly loses some of its moisture, which concentrates the flavours, and the smoke particles settle on the fish and help to seal in those flavours. John Wilson says, 'The craft of smoking and the mark of a good smoker is his ability to extract moisture from the fish and highlight the essential fish oils.'

The quality of smoked salmon depends upon the quality and freshness of the raw salmon, the salt used and the wood chosen for the smoke. Thin smoked salmon slices should be translucent when held up to the light and a uniform persimmon—orange colour. Good quality smoked salmon slices will separate easily.

SHORTCUT

John Wilson | Mohr Food

Try smoked salmon folded through softly scrambled eggs or served with baby rocket leaves and new season asparagus drizzled with extra virgin olive oil.

WIND- AND AIR-DRIED SALMON

Salmon fillets are first dry-cured with a mixture of sea salt and sugar. Some may be sprinkled with fresh herbs or other flavourings. They are left to cure for between 8 and 14 hours, during which time they are permeated with a subtle flavour from the cure. The fillets are

TASMANIA'S ATLANTIC SALMON

The Atlantic salmon farmed in Tasmania's isolated Esperance Bay has gained an international reputation for fine quality. Esperance Bay has clean, pure water and the fish are free of bacteria and disease — earning a disease-free status that is an achievement many other fish farming nations find hard to match. The harvest weight of a Tasmanian salmon is about 3.5 kilograms, which it reaches faster than anywhere else in the world due to the superior growing conditions in Tasmania. The fish are kept in large floating cages and are processed within minutes of leaving the water. The fresh salmon season is from September to March. For an industry that only started in 1984, Atlantic salmon growing in Tasmania has been a spectacular success.

MOHR FOOD
(Sydney, New South Wales)

Mohr Food dry cure their smoked salmon by hand using sea salt, raw sugar, fresh herbs, such as dill and coriander, and white pepper. The quality of the fish, the dry cure and the smoking gives the flesh of the fish an intense colour. Sel de Guérand, a natural unprocessed French marsh salt, is used with freshly grated horseradish for the cure of their air-dried salmon. They also make wind-dried salmon with Asian flavours; fresh lemon grass, coriander and kaffir lime leaves which infuse the fish with a subtle Asian flavour. The fillets are then rinsed and painted with a concentrated syrup made from kaffir lime leaves, lemon grass, fresh coriander, shallots and a trace of chilli before being wind-dried to bring the cure flavours together.

rinsed and air- or wind-dried for about 12 hours at an air temperature of around 20°C.

GRAVLAX

A Scandinavian specialty, gravlax was originally a side of salmon coated with salt and sugar and flavoured with crushed white peppercorns and lots of fresh dill. It was buried in the ground in winter (the name gravlax means 'grave salmon') and left to cure until spring. It was then eaten — the salt had cured it.

Nowadays gravlax is made in the same way, but not buried; it is simply weighted and refrigerated for 24–36 hours. Traditionally it is eaten with a mustard and dill sauce.

GRAVLAX OF SALMON, MASCARPONE, PINK EYE POTATO AND BABY CAPERS PIZZA

Glen Bowman | The Centennial Hotel
Serves 4

Pizza dough (see page 43)
2 pink eye potatoes, very thinly sliced
salt and freshly ground black pepper
3/4 cup mozzarella, grated
1/4 cup parmesan, grated
olive oil
5 slices gravlax
1 Spanish onion, peeled and thinly sliced
2 tablespoons baby salted capers, rinsed
2 tablespoons mascarpone

Roll out the dough on a lightly floured surface, then place it in a well oiled pizza pan. Arrange the potato slices on the base, season with salt and pepper, sprinkle with the mozzarella and parmesan and drizzle with olive oil.

Bake for approximately 15 to 20 minutes in a preheated 220°C oven or until the base is crisp. Arrange the gravlax on the pizza base then scatter the onion, capers and mascarpone over the top. To finish, drizzle with olive oil.

SHORTCUTS

Serve gravlax on blinis with a spoonful of crème fraîche.

Boil baby potatoes and serve with gravlax and a mustard and dill sauce.

SIMON SAYS: TRY AIR DRIED SALMON WITH HORSE-RADISH, HOT STEAMED BABY POTATOES AND A MIXED GREEN SALAD TOSSED WITH VINAIGRETTE.

SHORTCUT

Make a sugar syrup with palm sugar. Add lime juice, chopped shallots, chopped fresh coriander and finely chopped red chilli. Drizzle over slices of air- or wind-dried salmon and serve with a salad made with finely grated green papaya, chopped peanuts and fried green onions. Drizzle slices of the salmon with extra virgin olive oil and a little sauvignon blanc. Serve with toasted sourdough bread.

ANCHOVIES

Anchovies are caught throughout the world. They are a small, flavoursome oily fish. The best anchovies are lightly salted, cured, then hand filleted and packed in quality olive oil. An anchovy treated in this way is firm and succulent.

SIMON SAYS: I LIKE TO EAT ANCHOVIES ON THEIR OWN, SO THAT THEIR TASTE SHINES THROUGH: ON A SLICE OF GRILLED SOURDOUGH BREAD DRIZZLED WITH OLIVE OIL, OR WITH SPAGHETTI TOSSED WITH DICED GARLIC, OLIVE OIL AND FRESH CORIANDER — OR PUREE SEVERAL ANCHOVY FILLETS, MIX INTO AIOLI AND SERVE WITH GRILLED TUNA STEAKS.

SHORTCUT

Tony Bilson | Ampersand

Spread mashed potato over a shallow, buttered ovenproof dish. Lay anchovy fillets across the top, in a lattice-fashion. Sprinkle lightly with grated parmesan and nutmeg and bake at 180°C for 20–25 minutes.

BAGNA CAÔDA

180 ml olive oil
40g butter
2 cloves garlic, peeled and finely chopped
8–10 anchovy fillets, chopped
fresh raw vegetables (celery, carrot, cauliflower, broccoli, etc.), cut into batons
sourdough bread

Heat the oil and butter, add the garlic and sauté briefly. Add the anchovies and cook over a low heat, stirring until the anchovies have dissolved. Serve hot with raw vegetables and bread for dipping.

SHORTCUT

Anchovy butter

Mash three anchovies with the juice of a lemon and 100g unsalted butter. Season with freshly ground black pepper and put into little pots. Cover and refrigerate for up to one week. Use anchovy butter on grilled fish, potatoes, scrambled eggs and toast.

ANCHOIADE
Makes about 1 cup

Make an anchoiade for spreading on pieces of toast or as a dip for bread. Using a mortar and pestle, pound together about 12 anchovy fillets with two peeled cloves of garlic and a drop of vinegar, then add enough olive oil to make a coarse paste. Anchoiade can be refrigerated for about five days.

ORTIZ, SPAIN

Ortiz, one of the few processors of anchovies, retain the traditional methods used by the fishermen of Spain for hundreds of years. Ortiz sends boats out daily to fish for anchovies so that the fish are always freshly caught (unlike the fish processing boats which travel for up to three months to fish off South America and Africa). The fish are processed not more than eight hours after being taken from the water. They are placed in layers of sea salt for 12 to 24 hours, rinsed, then packed in salt again and cured for five months. The anchovies are then filleted by hand, rather than by machine, and packed in quality olive oil.

TUNA

Tuna is a meaty fish with a firm texture. Australia's finest tuna is exported to Japan where it commands exceptionally high prices. In recent years Australians have discovered how good tuna is and it is now sold fresh in our fish markets. Varieties that are sought after are the southern bluefin, which the Japanese prefer for sashimi; yellowfin tuna, also popular for sashimi; skipjack and the albacore, most highly regarded in the USA.

Good quality tinned tuna retains the meaty texture that fresh tuna has—it is firm and comes in thick fillets; the best part of the tuna comes from the belly of the fish. Top quality tuna is line caught (no dolphins get trapped in the nets, and the fish suffers less trauma), bled and cooked in a herbed brine. Then it is filleted and canned in very good quality olive oil with a judicious amount of wine vinegar.

Use tinned tuna in a niçoise salad or make the ultimate tuna sandwich.

NIÇOISE SALAD
Serves 4

leaves of 2–3 baby cos lettuces
125g green beans, blanched
1 punnet of cherry tomatoes, halved
1/2 teaspoon sea salt
5 tablespoons extra virgin olive oil
8 hard-boiled eggs, shelled and halved
150g small black Ligurian olives
100g anchovy fillets
125g tuna in olive oil, drained and broken into chunks

Put the lettuce, beans, tomatoes, sea salt and olive oil in a salad bowl. Toss until the salad is coated with olive oil. Add the remaining ingredients and toss gently to combine, bringing some of the olives, tuna, tomatoes and eggs to the top.

SQUID INK

Squid ink, which is contained in a little sac in both cuttlefish and squid, was originally used as sepia ink in Roman paintings. The sweetest ink comes from the cuttlefish, but both inks can be used to darken and enrich a sauce for pasta or to make the Italian classic risotto nero (black rice). Cuttlefish has a white bone inside it and is shorter and rounder than squid. The ink is extracted from the cuttlefish by removing the ink sacs from the fish and draining them. Quite a lot of ink sacs are required; about 500g of cuttlefish produces enough ink to make a risotto nero for four people.

CAVIAR

Caviar is the eggs of the sturgeon, a large, ancient fish that lives in the Caspian Sea. A most prized delicacy, it is even more of a rarity now that over-fishing in the Caspian Sea, the Black Sea and the Gironde River has resulted in a depletion of sturgeon. The female beluga sturgeon must be 15–20 years old before her eggs can be harvested, so it is not an industry that can recover quickly once supplies run low. The future for the harvesting of caviar lies with farmed sturgeon.

The three different types of caviar are named for the fish from which the eggs are taken. Beluga caviar, the most expensive and largest in size, comes from the giant short-nosed sturgeon, which can grow to 4 metres in length and live to be 100. The roe is light grey to black in colour, has a distinctive 'eye' and can be 2.5 to 3 millimetres in diameter. Osietra caviar comes from a smaller fish, but it is still 2 metres in length. The caviar pearls are small and grey/brown with tinges of gold, and the flavour is very delicate. The sevruga sturgeon grows to a metre and a half long. It is the least rare of the three fish as it matures in seven years. The caviar is the smallest of the three and is gun-metal grey to black. It has an aromatic flavour and the eggs are soft and creamy on the palate.

Caviar should have a subtle saline flavour, without tasting fishy. The pearls should be firm, whole and well oiled. The size and colour are to do with the time of year that the fish is caught, the maturity of the eggs and how close it is to spawning — the eggs are darker the nearer to spawning. The size of the caviar pearls is a matter of preference, as is colour.

Once the eggs are harvested, washed and drained, they are graded and salted. The higher the quality of the eggs, the less salt is used (these are labelled 'malossol', meaning little salt). After salting, the eggs are drained, packed into cans, refrigerated and sent to destinations all over the world. Caviar can be pasteurised for longer life. However, the pearls become leathery and the flavour complexity is lost.

The high cost of caviar relates to the scarcity of sturgeon, the time it takes for the female to produce eggs, the difficulty of catching the fish, and processing and transporting caviar because it is so perishable. Until sturgeon becomes a farmed fish caviar will remain scarce.

Caviar should be refrigerated and kept sealed until it is served. It is very delicate and begins to oxidise with exposure to air, which affects the texture of the caviar. It is available both fresh and pasteurised. Fresh caviar will keep unopened in the refrigerator for up to three months. Once opened it can be kept for about three days. Pasteurised caviar is less fragile and will keep unopened for up to 18 months in the refrigerator.

The ideal caviar is plump and moist, with each individual pearl shiny, smooth, separate and softly intact. When you take a spoonful in your mouth and gently press the pearls against your palate, they should very briefly resist and then burst to release an intense flavour. One of the pleasures of eating caviar is to feel the little explosion in your mouth as you crush the pearls.

Caviar should not come into contact with metal: a mother of pearl caviar spoon is the ideal implement.

SIMON SAYS: IN RUSSIA IT IS TRADITIONAL TO DRINK ICED VODKA WITH CAVIAR, BUT THE IDEAL ACCOMPANIMENT IS A GLASS OF CHILLED CHAMPAGNE.

Caviar was introduced to the French by two enterprising Russian brothers, Melkom and Mougcheg Petrossian. Having escaped to Paris during the Russian Revolution, they saw a gap in the market — there was no caviar in Paris. The Union of Socialist Soviet Republics urgently needed cash, there was no shortage of sturgeon, and a deal was struck: the brothers could import fine Russian caviar into France. The problem now was how to get Parisians to acquire a taste for it. The brothers set up a stand in the Gastronomic Exhibition at the Grand Palais in 1920 and offered free caviar tastings. They were forced to install spittoons because even though plenty of people tasted it, most of them hated it. There were exceptions, however, and by the end of the exhibition, caviar had been established in Paris as a new luxury food.

FLYING FISH ROE

Flying fish are found throughout the world's oceans, including the regions of the Pacific. Flying fish roe has traditionally been used in Japanese cuisine but is now available worldwide. The roe has a slightly fishy flavour and crunchy texture when compared to caviar.

SALMON ROE

Salmon roe is not graded in the same way as caviar, which simplifies the processing procedure. Salmon can be milked for their roe when the eggs have matured sufficiently, which can be done without the destruction of the fish. The colour ranges from golden to reddish amber to reddish orange. The eggs are three to four times larger than beluga caviar and have the characteristic pop as the eggs are rolled between the tongue and palate. The taste is not as subtle and more piquant than caviar.

CANAPES

Place a dollop of crème fraîche on a witlof leaf and top with salmon roe.

Place $^1/_2$ teaspoon of crème fraîche on a slice of cucumber and top with salmon roe.

Make blinis (or tiny pancakes) and top with sour cream and flying fish roe.

SMOKED TROUT AND CELERIAC SALAD WITH MAYONNAISE AND FLYING FISH ROE

Alex Herbert

Serves 4

200g smoked trout, flaked
3 cups grated celeriac, tossed in a little lemon juice
4 tablespoons chives, chopped
4 tablespoons Italian parsley, torn
4 tablespoons white onion, peeled and finely diced
1 tablespoon cornichons, finely sliced
1 $^1/_2$ teaspoons lemon juice
8 tablespoons mayonnaise
4 tablespoons flying fish roe

In a large bowl, toss gently together the trout, celeriac, chives, parsley, onion and cornichons. Mix in the lemon juice and mayonnaise and assemble into mounds on four plates. Sprinkle each salad with flying fish roe before serving.

OYSTERS

Oysters have been gathered since ancient times and oyster shells have been found in Aboriginal middens around the Australian coastline. Natural oyster beds are found along our shores and estuaries, while oysters have been farmed in Australia for many years. The most commonly farmed oyster was the Sydney rock oyster but the Pacific oyster, which can be grown in nearly half the time, is now farmed in almost equal numbers.

ROCK OYSTERS OR SYDNEY ROCK OYSTERS are native to Australia. They grow over a period of 30 to 40 months and are found from Hervey Bay in Queensland right down the east coast to Victoria. They are a golden–green colour and have a rich flavour with a long aftertaste. They are farmed in places such as the Hawkesbury River, Shoalhaven River and Merimbula.

PACIFIC OYSTERS are native to Japan. Their growth is more rapid than the Sydney rock oyster, taking only 18 to 24 months to mature. Grown mainly in Tasmania and South Australia, they are a metallic grey colour and have a clean flavour and finish with a creamy texture. They are farmed in places such as Streaky Bay, Coffin Bay and Kangaroo Island in South Australia and Freycinet, Oyster Bay and Pittwater in Tasmania. Oyster sprat are produced at a rate of over 60 million a year in Tasmania for shipment to oyster farmers in Tasmania and South Australia.

FLAVOUR

Clean unpolluted water and good tidal flow is extremely important for growing oysters. Temperature is also important. If the oyster is too cold its shell will grow and not the meat inside, and if it is too warm the oyster can become stressed and even die. The oyster is a bivalve and breathes and eats simultaneously, filtering the water and feeding on the fungi and algae flowing by. Oysters should be plump and shiny, a natural creamy colour with a clear liquor, and fresh smelling. If still in their shells, the shells should be tightly closed.

SHORTCUT
Janni Kyritsis | MG Garage

Divide 3 whole heads of garlic into cloves, leaving one layer of skin on. Gently cook in a covered pan with 100g butter and 50 ml olive oil for 10–15 minutes, until soft. Cool, then peel and dice the garlic and return to the oil and butter. Season to taste. Remove 12 oysters and any liquid from their shells and mix with the garlic. Heat the oyster shells until piping hot and replace the oysters in the shells. Serve sprinkled with breadcrumbs toasted in a little butter.

CHARCUTERIE

EARLY TRIBES DRIED THEIR LEFT-OVER MEAT IN THE SUN. OVER THOUSANDS OF YEARS THIS simple METHOD HAS EVOLVED INTO A WIDE REPERTOIRE OF PRESERVING TECHNIQUES THAT INCLUDE DRYING, SMOKING AND SALTING IN A DIVERSE RANGE OF COMBINATIONS. IN THE process OF DISCOVERING NEW WAYS OF KEEPING MEAT IN TIMES OF PLENTY FOR LEANER DAYS AHEAD, THE RAW PRODUCT MOVED INTO NEW DIMENSIONS OF TASTE AND TEXTURE — A CASE OF MAKING A virtue OF NECESSITY. MOST OF THE PRESERVED MEATS WE ENJOY TODAY DEVELOPED AS european REGIONAL SPECIALTIES, HEARTY PEASANT FARE TO SATISFY BIG APPETITES. THE BASICS OF CHARCUTERIE ARE QUALITY HAMS, SMOKED MEATS, SAUSAGES, TERRINES, PATES AND CONFIT.

HAM

A ham usually refers to the back legs of a pig, salted and cooked, air dried or smoked. However, front legs and shoulders prepared in the same way are often also referred to as 'ham'. The taste of ham is dependent on the breed of pig, its age, its diet and how it lived (i.e. active or sedentary). It also depends on its curing.

Curing is done either by frequent rubbing with salt, or by immersion in a brine bath. The traditional production of ham depends heavily on the brine used. The correct brine solution and application of the brine is indispensable to a good quality artisan ham. The brine is a mixture of water, salt and other ingredients such as sugar. Seasonings can be important too in order to give the ham a special flavour — these can include bay leaves, thyme, garlic, peppercorns, cloves and spices. An example is York ham, which is usually cured in a mild brine for 40–60 days, depending on the size of the ham. The ham is then drained and air dried for 36–48 hours and finally cooked in a well-flavoured bouillon.

AIR-DRIED HAMS

Dried hams are one of the oldest of the charcuterie products. Today's technological advances make drying a much more predictable art than it was in earlier times. Before refrigeration, hams were prepared and dried during the cool winter months to maintain a cool even temperature.

An air-dried ham is generally cured by rubbing salt into the ham, then immersing the ham entirely in a bed of salt. The duration of the salting depends on the weight of the ham, but an indication is three days for each kilogram. Once every 5–6 days the ham is withdrawn from the salt and rubbed vigorously with a special rubbing salt, then it is replaced in the bed of salt. At the end of this process the ham is removed to a cool place for about 15 days, which allows the salt to further penetrate the meat. The ham is soaked in cold running water, to eliminate the surface salt, and hung to drain. Hams prepared in this way are dried at 12–14°C and 75–80 per cent humidity for four months to one year. Air-dried hams include Parma ham from Italy, *jamón serrano* (mountain ham) from Spain and *jamón de Toulouse* from France.

SMOKED HAM

For hams that are smoked rather than dried, the wood that is chosen for smoking has a direct effect on the flavour of the ham: the famous Westphalian ham of Germany is smoked over ash or beech with a touch of juniper and Virginia ham is smoked over hickory and apple-wood.

Some hams, for example Parma ham, are eaten uncooked; other hams, such as York ham, are always cooked.

BAKED HAM

Joan Campbell
Serves 12

1 cooked leg ham
1 x 440g can pineapple juice
1/4 cup sherry
500g brown sugar
prepared mustard
powdered cloves

Preheat the oven to 150°C. Put the pineapple juice, sherry and brown sugar in a saucepan and cook to a syrup.

Carefully remove the skin from the ham and rub in the prepared mustard to colour the fat a pale yellow. Dust with powdered cloves. Place the ham in a large baking tin and pour the syrup around the ham, not over the top. Cook on the bottom shelf of the oven for 30 minutes, then, basting frequently with the syrup, cook for a further 60 minutes. Serve hot or cold.

ROASTED TOMATO AND BULB FENNEL SOUP

Leigh Stone Herbert
Serves 6

1 tablespoon olive oil
10 ripe roma tomatoes, washed and drained
1 leek, washed and chopped
1 small bulb of fennel, trimmed and chopped
6 thin slices prosciutto
focaccia
olive oil, extra
thyme, basil or sage, chopped
1 clove garlic, chopped
salt and freshly ground pepper

Heat a roasting pan in the oven at 230°C, then remove from the oven and put over a medium heat. Add the olive oil and toss in the dry tomatoes rolling them around in the hot oil until they are well coated. Return the pan to the oven and roast the tomatoes, turning occasionally until their skins begin to blacken. Add the remaining vegetables and roast until soft. Remove from the oven and cool.

Gently grill the prosciutto until crisp. Cool on kitchen paper. Cut the focaccia into small croutons, toss in the extra olive oil and bake in the oven until golden brown.

When cool enough, peel the tomatoes. Place the peeled tomatoes into a food processor with the herbs, leek, fennel and garlic. Coarsely chop, then remove half the mixture and set aside. Purée the remaining mixture. Combine the mixtures and season with salt and pepper. When ready to serve, gently heat the mixture in a saucepan.

To serve, ladle into large warmed bowls and carefully spoon a pool of olive oil onto the surface. Sprinkle with more of your favourite herb and serve with the grilled prosciutto and focaccia croutons. The soup can also be served chilled in hot weather.

PROSCIUTTO — ITALIAN HAM

Prosciutto is still made in the time-honoured way — the traditional process of salting a ham and hanging it to dry for up to a year. The most well-known Italian prosciutti are produced in two regions — Fruili and Parma. Traditionally, the pigs of Fruili foraged around the bottom of oak trees and a major component of their diet was acorns; whereas the pigs of Parma were fed on the whey left over from the making of parmesan cheese, giving the two resulting prosciutti very different flavours. The prosciutto made in Parma, *prosciutto di Parma*, is the most famous Italian air-dried ham.

PROSCIUTTO FRESCO is raw ham; **PROSCIUTTO COTTO** is cooked ham; **PROSCIUTTO CRUDO** literally means 'raw ham', however, this is the prosciutto that one eats — the salt-cured, air-dried ham. Prosciutto is never smoked. Prosciutto can be eaten on its own, as part of an antipasto, with melon or mozzarella or figs, or it can be used in cooking. It should be sliced very thinly.

There are five types of pancetta:

PANCETTA ARROTOLATA
(meaning rolled) which is the
common pancetta;

PANCETTA AFFUMICATA
or smoked;

PANCETTA STESA
(meaning spread out) which is a
slab of bacon that has been
salted;

PANCETTA FRESCA, or
raw bacon; and

PANCETTA COPPATA
which is rolled with coppa and
eaten as a cold meat like salami
or prosciutto.

SWEET CORN FRITTERS WITH ROAST TOMATO AND BACON

Bill Granger | bills
Makes 16

Fritter batter:
2 cups plain flour
1 teaspoon baking powder
2 tablespoons sugar
3 eggs
1 cup milk
1/2 teaspoon salt
1/2 teaspoon paprika

Vegetables:
2 cups corn kernels
1/2 cup red capsicum, diced
1/2 cup spring onions, chopped
1/4 cup coriander and parsley, chopped

To serve:
1 bunch rocket, washed and dried
grilled bacon, 2 rashers per person
roast tomatoes, 2 halves per person

TO MAKE THE FRITTER BATTER: Whisk all the ingredients
together until they form a stiff batter.

Mix the vegetables and herbs together in a mixing bowl, then add
just enough batter to lightly bind them. Do not mix the vegetables
in the fritter batter more than one hour before you are ready to use
them as the salt in the batter draws out the liquid in the vegetables
and they will become soggy.

Heat 2 tablespoons of oil in a non-stick pan until hot, then drop
large tablespoons of fritter mix into the pan. Reduce the heat and
cook until the underside of each fritter is golden. Turn over and
cook on the other side.

TO SERVE: Place one fritter on a plate and top with some rocket
leaves, two rashers of bacon and two tomato halves. Place a second
fritter on top.

PANCETTA

Pancetta is the same cut as bacon, except that it is not smoked. The slab of bacon is rolled up into a salami shape around seasonings of pepper and herbs to make it more flavoursome. It is left to air dry to allow the flavours to infuse. The meat is quite fatty but it is usually cut thinly to use in cooking. When it is good quality it can be eaten as it is, like any other cold meat. It can be used as a flavouring in cooking and makes excellent lardons.

SIMON SAYS: THREAD ALTERNATE CUBES OF PANCETTA AND LEAN VEAL WITH SAGE LEAVES AND ROSEMARY SPRIGS ON SKEWERS TO BARBECUE.

SAUSAGES

A well made sausage is a treat whether it is served with mashed potato and grainy mustard or barbecued and sandwiched in a piece of bread. Sausages exist in nearly all cuisines and there are sausages to please almost everyone, from peasant-style aromatic to delicately spiced.

The process of sausage making evolved as an effort to economise and make use of whatever scraps of meat were left over after an animal had been butchered. The procedure of stuffing meat into casings remains basically unchanged today, but sausage making is a highly respected culinary art. It is impossible to estimate how many different types of sausages exist, with every culture having its own varieties and variations.

The best sausages contain the more flavoursome cuts of meat, which may be coarsely or finely minced. They also contain fat, a necessary ingredient in a sausage, which serves three purposes: adding flavour, binding the mixture of meat and seasonings, and providing moisture.

SAUSAGES

SMOKED SAUSAGES are made from meats that have been cured and then smoked over wood fires. They can be either cooked or uncooked (frankfurters).

COOKED SAUSAGES (liverwurst, mortadella, garlic sausage) are made from meats that are either fresh or preserved by curing.

FRESH SAUSAGES are made from ground meats that have not been cooked or cured.

DRIED SAUSAGES are made from fresh meats that have been spiced then dried for varying periods of time.

Most sausages are made with pork, although veal, chicken, duck, beef and lamb sausages are also available, as well as combinations of different meats. Depending on the sausage, a range of flavourings can be added such as herbs, spices, onions, garlic, nuts and alcohol. Sausages can be fresh, precooked, air dried or smoked.

Sausage skins were traditionally made from the intestines of sheep and pigs, and the best sausages still use natural casings.

Some of the better known sausages that are available include:

ANDOUILLES (FRENCH): Pork sausages seasoned with pepper, salt, nutmeg, ginger and cinnamon and sometimes bay leaves, onions and mushrooms.

BLACK PUDDING (ENGLISH): Blood sausage made with beef blood, barley, oatmeal and flour and flavoured with onions, salt, pepper, coriander, celery seeds, mustard and allspice.

BOLOGNA (ITALIAN): A mixture of beef and pork, often seasoned with sage, cayenne, paprika, salt and black pepper.

BOUDIN BLANC (FRENCH): A white sausage usually made from pork or chicken, cream and light seasoning — sometimes truffles are added.

BOUDIN NOIR (FRENCH): A type of blood sausage usually made with pork, blood, suet, eggs, cream, onions, brandy and spices.

BRATWURST (GERMAN): Veal and pork seasoned with ginger, mustard and coriander.

CALABRESE SALAMI (ITALIAN): Pork seasoned heavily with hot pepper and garlic, then air dried.

CERVELAT (FRENCH): Lean pork spiced with parsley, thyme, basil, nutmeg and cloves, and sometimes pimiento. The sausages are tied in lengths and dried.

CEVAPCICI (YUGOSLAVIAN): Skinless beef and veal spiced with garlic, parsley and paprika.

CHIPOLATA (SPANISH): A small fresh sausage.

CHORIZO (SPANISH): Beef and pork seasoned with hot pepper, garlic, salt, chilli, sugar, vinegar and sometimes pimiento. Can be fresh, smoked or dried.

COTECHINO (ITALIAN): Pork sausage flavoured with nutmeg, cloves, garlic, coriander and hot pepper.

FLEISCHWURST (GERMAN): All beef, or pork and beef flavoured with garlic, paprika, salt and pepper and lightly smoked.

KABANOS (POLISH) Smoked pork and beef flavoured with garlic and mace.

LIVERWURST (GERMAN): Pork liver sausage seasoned with salt, white pepper, allspice and onion.

LYON SAUSAGE (FRENCH): Well-trimmed pork mixed with salt pork, salt, pepper, garlic and white peppercorns. They are large and are dried for several months.

METTWURST (GERMAN): A form of liverwurst but made from finely ground pork liver.

PORK SAUSAGE (ENGLISH): Equal portions of lean and fat pork seasoned with mustard, allspice, mace, cayenne, ginger, salt and pepper. Rice and breadcrumbs are added as fillers.

SAUCISSES DE CAMPAGNE (FRENCH): Coarse pork and pork fat flavoured with wine, ginger, cinnamon, nutmeg and garlic.

SAUCISSON CERVELAT (FRENCH): Coarsely chopped pork and pork fat sausages, smoked for up to five days.

TOULOUSE SAUSAGE (FRENCH): The sausage made famous in cassoulet. Pork neck or shoulder mixed with fat and seasoned lightly with salt, sugar, white pepper, white wine and garlic.

Poach a pork saucisson gently in water and serve it sliced with a hot potato salad made with waxy potatoes such as pink eye or desirée, tossed gently with an aïoli made from garlic-infused oil.

SIMON SAYS: COOK SAUSAGES SLOWLY EITHER IN A PAN, IN THE OVEN, OR ON THE BARBECUE. SOME SAUSAGES, ESPECIALLY THE SAUCISSON LYONNAISE TYPE (SIMPLE PORK SAUSAGE) RETAIN THEIR FLAVOUR AND JUICINESS BEST WHEN GENTLY POACHED.

SALAMI

Salami is an Italian specialty made from pork and seasonings then air dried for a few months. Traditionally it was made when the weather became cool and the salamis could dry through the cold of winter at a constant temperature. The pig is chosen and butchered, the meat is minced and mixed with seasonings, the salami cases are filled and tied off and the finished salamis are hung in an airy dry place to mature.

COTECHINO AND FENNEL BROTH

Chris Taylor | Fraser's
Serves 8

1 onion, peeled and diced
1 large fennel bulb, trimmed and diced
4 stalks heart of celery, diced
3 cloves garlic, peeled and crushed
200g butternut pumpkin, peeled and diced
3 sprigs thyme
extra virgin olive oil
1 litre chicken stock
100g black eye beans, soaked overnight
1 cotechino (large enough to serve 8)
salt and freshly ground pepper
50g silverbeet, white stalks removed
parmesan cheese, shaved

Sweat the onion, fennel, celery, garlic, pumpkin and thyme with the olive oil for 5 minutes. Add the chicken stock. Bring to the boil and add the black eye beans, then turn down and simmer for 15–20 minutes or until tender.

Put the cotechino in 2 litres of boiling water for 15–20 minutes to remove excess fat. Take the cotechino out of the water and dry with a cloth. Add the whole sausage to the soup and let it sit in the soup until ready to serve.

To serve, take the cotechino out of the soup, remove the skin and slice thinly. Season the soup to taste. Cook the silverbeet. Pour the soup into bowls, making sure there are more vegetables than liquid. Place the silverbeet on the vegetables with three slices of cotechino. Place some shaved parmesan on top and drizzle extra virgin olive oil around the soup.

FOIE GRAS

Foie gras is the oversized liver of a fattened duck or goose and is one of the great delicacies of France; the best come from Alsace and Périgord.

Thousands of years ago it was noticed how wild geese would gorge themselves in preparation for their long migratory flights. The hunted geese were discovered to have a fattened, enlarged liver which would sustain the birds during their flight. This was a great delicacy and the natural process was soon imitated by force feeding geese and ducks. The best goose livers weigh from 500–700g and are rich in fat and very fragile; however, duck livers are becoming the more common because the bird is quicker to mature, easier to handle and duck meat is in demand.

Fresh foie gras needs to have the lobes separated and, like most liver, any blood vessels need to be removed with a sharp knife. Fresh foie gras needs to be consumed soon after purchase.

ESCALOPE OF FOIE GRAS 'EN AIGRE DOUX'

Tony Bilson | Ampersand
Serves 4

12 baby turnips, trimmed and halved
1 leek, trimmed, halved and cut into 5 mm ribbons
1 x 400–500g mi-cut (see below) or fresh foie gras
salt and freshly ground pepper
1 tablespoon reduced veal or poultry stock
2 tablespoons shaved truffle (optional)

Sauce:
150 ml good vintage port
100 ml sherry vinegar

Cook the turnips in boiling salted water for five minutes or until just tender. Drain and refresh under cold water. Blanch the leek in boiling salted water.

Heat the vegetables in a steamer and set aside. Cut the foie gras into 1.5 cm thick slices and season with salt and pepper. Heat a heavy skillet over a medium flame and cook the foie gras on each side for one minute or until slightly browned. Remove with a slotted spatula and drain on kitchen paper. Set the skillet aside.

TO MAKE THE SAUCE: Bring the port and vinegar to the boil in a small saucepan and reduce to a syrup.

Arrange the leek in the centre of warmed plates and space the turnips evenly around it. Lay the foie gras on the bed of leeks.

Deglaze the skillet with the port/vinegar syrup, the stock and the truffle. Spoon the resulting vinaigrette made from the liquids and the remaining fat in the pan over the foie gras.

PRESERVED FOIE GRAS

THE MI-CUT, or lightly preserved, foie gras is the most refined and least-cooked. It is steamed at 75°C and sealed. It should be consumed within four weeks.

THE SEMI-CONSERVE, or semi-preserved, foie gras is gently and

slowly cooked in a closed container. The juices that are lost during cooking are absorbed back into the liver, keeping it succulent. The term semi-cooked doesn't mean that it is half cooked; it simply means it has been cooked at a very low temperature which preserves it.

Provided the seal is not broken and it is stored properly, the liver can be kept for six months.

FOIE GRAS DE CONSERVE or preserved foie gras is cooked at 100°C which sterilises it. It is tinned and has a long shelf life.

FOIE GRAS IN ASPIC is goose liver cooked in stock. The whole foie gras is placed in a glass jar, salt and spices are added, and it is covered with stock. It is cooked and when it cools the stock sets into a natural jelly. Serve on little pieces of hot toast.

PATE DE FOIE GRAS is puréed goose liver to which pork liver or truffles may have been added.

PUREE DE FOIE GRAS is a mousseline made with at least 55 per cent goose liver.

GOOSE FAT

This excellent cooking fat can be heated to about 200°C before it burns and imparts its characteristic flavour to any food cooked in it. It is also used in the making of confit — a classic method of meat preservation in France. A confit in its ideal form consists of wings, thighs, legs or breasts of goose or duck preserved in its own fat. Goose fat alone or as a part of a confit has a natural role to play in cassoulet, one of the famous French dishes from Languedoc, a substantial dish of haricot beans and meats cooked slowly.

SIMON SAYS: THERE'S NO BETTER WAY TO SAUTÉ POTATOES THAN IN GOOSE FAT. PREPARED GOOSE FAT MAKES A CONFIT EASIER; IT SAVES HAVING TO RENDER AND CLARIFY THE FAT YOURSELF.

CONFIT DUCK LEGS

Dany Chouet | Cleopatra
Makes 12 servings

12 duck legs, whole Maryland
1 bunch fresh thyme
1 branch fresh rosemary
1 bay leaf, crushed
2 garlic cloves, crushed
1–2 cups sea salt, freshly ground pepper and nutmeg
2 kg rendered duck or goose fat

Confit duck legs may be preserved in the refrigerator for up to two months as long as they are completely covered with duck fat and no air bubbles remain.

Clean the duck legs, but leave all fat on them. Strip the leaves from the stems of the thyme and rosemary and discard the stems. Combine the thyme, rosemary, bay leaf and garlic. Place the duck legs in a large mixing bowl or large plastic container. Rub them on both sides with the herb mixture and season with salt and equal amounts of freshly ground pepper and nutmeg.

Cover tightly and leave in the refrigerator overnight or preferably for 24 hours.

The next day, melt the duck fat in a large saucepan or casserole dish over a very low heat. Meanwhile, remove the legs one by one and thoroughly wipe dry with kitchen paper. When the fat is just warm, but not boiling, plunge the legs carefully in the pot. Cook very slowly, barely simmering, for 2–3 hours. The confit is cooked when easily pierced by a wooden skewer. Remove the duck legs from the pot and arrange in a ceramic or strong plastic dish. When the fat is lukewarm, pour it through a fine sieve over the meat. When it has thoroughly cooled, cover and place in the refrigerator.

PATE/TERRINES/MOUSSELINES

Country terrines, pâtés, galantines, pork pies and brawns have been the staples of the European farmhouse kitchen for centuries. Their production grew from the need to use every scrap of meat, game or fish that was available.

TERRINES AND PATES: Terrines and pâtés are generally fairly interchangeable terms today but in early times there was a much greater distinction.

The pastry crusts of early pâtés were designed for durability first and foremost so as to easily transport the pâté — keeping the meats inside the pastry safe and free from contamination.

The name terrine comes from the deep earthenware dish that terrines are traditionally cooked in. Terrines can be made of meat or fish. Fish terrines are usually fine purées or mousselines of fish or shellfish. (A mousseline is a mildly flavoured and smooth textured purée bound with egg white and enriched with cream.) Meat terrines can be veal, rabbit, game or offal. Whatever meats are used, pork is most often part of the mixture because it blends unobtrusively with other meats and spices and seasonings.

To achieve a moist richness these dishes must have a generous amount of fat. For preparations served cold, pork fat is the usual choice because it retains a firm, smooth texture and white colour when it is cooked. It is also a good preservative, acting in the same way as a confit. The pork fat is rendered and poured over a cooked terrine or pâté to form an airtight seal that retards spoilage.

To vary the colour and flavour, ingredients like coarsely chopped pistachio nuts, whole green peppercorns or pieces of truffle are added or layered. Many terrines are made by lining the dish with pork fat to keep the meat moist and are cooked covered in a bath of hot water to give a slow gentle heat.

GALANTINE: A galantine is made with meats or vegetables suspended in a gelatinous stock. The jelly or aspic is made from meats that are a good source of gelatine, such as veal knuckle, chicken wing tips and pig's trotters. The secret to the success of the dish is to slowly and gently poach the meats.

CHICKEN LIVER PARFAIT

Genevieve Copeland | Bonne Femme
Serves 6

1 kg chicken livers
200 ml olive oil
300g unsalted butter
200 ml brandy
4 rashers rindless bacon, diced
3 sprigs thyme, finely chopped
3 cloves garlic, crushed
1/2 onion, diced
salt and freshly ground black pepper
200 ml cream

Clean the chicken livers of any sinew. Heat a large frying pan with a little olive oil and butter. When the pan is almost smoking, place in enough chicken livers to coat the base of the pan. Do not overcrowd or the chicken livers will sweat rather than sear. Quickly sauté until they are just medium rare and still quite bouncy to touch. Add part of the brandy and flame. Pour the livers into a plastic tray. Repeat this process until all the livers are sealed.

In another pan sauté the bacon, thyme, garlic and onion in a little butter until softened. Process the livers, bacon, thyme, garlic and onion and the remainder of the butter and the salt and pepper until smooth. Add the cream and process again.

Pour into a drum sieve over a large bowl and rub through with a rubber spatula. Pour the sieved mixture into terrine moulds. Bang the air out to remove any bubbles and cover with plastic wrap. Refrigerate for at least six hours. Unmould and slice with a hot knife.

FROMAGERIE

CHEESE HAS BEEN DESCRIBED AS AN inspired COLLABORATION BETWEEN MAN AND NATURE. MADE FROM ONE BASIC INGREDIENT, MILK, IT'S AMAZINGLY versatile: A PERFECT FOOD WHEN EATEN ON ITS OWN OR IN PARTNERSHIP WITH OTHER INGREDIENTS. CHEESEMAKING HAD ITS BEGINNINGS THOUSANDS OF YEARS AGO WITH THE NEED FOR SURPLUS MILK TO BE KEPT FOR CONSUMPTION AT A LATER TIME. THE SIMPLE form THAT CHEESE FIRST TOOK WAS THE REMOVAL OF MOST OF THE WHEY OR LIQUID FROM THE MILK, LEAVING THE curds OR MILK SOLIDS. MOST OF THE CHEESE MADE IN THE VERY EARLIEST TIMES WOULD HAVE BEEN SIMPLE CURD CHEESES PRODUCED IN SMALL QUANTITIES AND CONSUMED SOON AFTER IT WAS MADE. EARLY farmers EVOLVED THE rudimentary CHEESEMAKING PRINCIPLES THAT STILL STAND TODAY. THEY DEVELOPED METHODS TO MAKE LONG-LASTING CHEESES OUT OF THEIR HERD'S SUMMER MILK SO THAT THE CHEESE COULD BE CONSUMED THROUGHOUT THE LONG WINTERS. AS TIME WENT ON THE FARMERS experimented AND SOON EACH REGION WAS MAKING ITS OWN STYLES OF CHEESES.

CHEESEMAKING

The industrial revolution transformed cheesemaking and over the ensuing 200 years factory-made cheese has, along with the introduction of refrigeration and modern technology, dominated cheesemaking. The arts of the traditional cheesemaker, however, have never been lost and the specialist cheese they produce is of ever greater interest as palates become sophisticated. There is an ever-widening variety of cheeses available and each has its own fundamental difference from another, whether it is the type of milk, the climate and pasture or the method of cheesemaking.

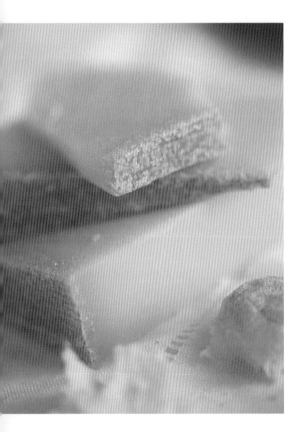

The quality of the milk is all-important in cheesemaking; traditional farmhouse cheesemakers have their own herds of cows, goats or sheep. Others rely on a number of local farmers or local dairies to supply them.

Interestingly, wherever specialist foods are produced, as with fine wines, the 'terroir' is an important component. The pastures and feed, the seasons and the health of the animals all play a part in the production of quality milk.

Cheesemaking, especially in the drier and milder climate of Australia, is influenced by seasons, with early and late spring and autumn producing the best milk and the cold of winter and the heat of summer producing the least. Farmhouse cheesemakers can control the quality of their milk throughout the seasons by controlling their animals' feed which reflects in the quality of the milk.

Cheese is made from milk, but a whole range of animals

produce milk suitable for cheesemaking besides cows — goats, sheep and buffalo. The properties of milk vary enormously depending on the animal; for instance, goat's milk has less lactose than does cow's, ewe's or buffalo milk. The balance of each animal's milk is suited to different types of cheesemaking.

COW'S MILK is the most widely used for cheesemaking in the Western world and for good reason: cows yield the most milk per animal at about 20 litres per day. Their milk is used to make the large volume, factory-made cheese but farmhouse and specialist cheese-makers also use cow's milk.

GOAT'S MILK is very delicate and can easily be tainted. Fresh milk is the very best starting point for making goat's cheese. But dairy goats produce far less milk than cows with only about 3 or 4 litres a day from one goat and then only when it is lactating. As well lactation in goats is very sensitive to weather changes.

EWE'S MILK has been used in the Middle East for thousands of years and in Europe for centuries. Notably roquefort and pecorino are both traditionally made from ewe's milk. Ewe's milk is richer than cow's or goat's milk, but a ewe only produces a tiny fraction of the milk a cow does. Ewes also only lactate for about two to three months a year. Ewe's milk is excellent when used for blue cheese, feta and pecorino as well as fresh cheese and yoghurt.

BUFFALO MILK has been used traditionally in Italy to make soft fresh cheeses like mozzarella and in Asia for yoghurt and fresh cheeses. Buffalo cows produce less than half the daily milk of a dairy cow but can lactate for most of the year — much longer than an ordinary dairy cow.

PURRUMBETE'S BUFFALO HERD

(Western Victoria)
Cheesemakers: Andrew & Thea Royal

Purrumbete in Victoria's western district is the first cheesemaking farm to introduce buffalo into Australia purely for its milk. More than 50 buffalo have been specially imported from Campania in southern Italy. Buffalo like a warm climate, and to overcome the cold of winter the buffalo herd is housed in large open sheds. The milk is used to make cheese and yoghurt and buffalo mozzarella. Buffalo mozzarella is new to Australia but has been made in the south of Italy for hundreds of years. It is regarded in Italy as the only true mozzarella, with cow's milk mozzarella seen as a poor imitation.

MAKING CHEESE

Not unlike wine, cheese is fermented to allow the microbes to do the preservative work. The art of the cheesemaker, like the winemaker, is to use their experience, skill and good judgment to create a great cheese from the raw materials. Like the making of wine (where the sugars in wine are converted to alcohol which preserves and stabilises the wine), cheese is basically made by converting the milk sugars (lactose) into lactic acid, which preserves and stabilises the curd. Salt is an important part of cheesemaking as with wine which uses sulphur to halt any further fermentation. Salt is used to halt the action of the lactic bacteria and, as with other foods, salt enhances the flavour and acts as a preservative.

The culture that is used to start the fermentation of milk is called a starter, and these bacterias are now carefully developed for the type of cheese to be made and are an exacting part of today's cheesemaking.

Naturally ripened cheese is a living organism that is constantly undergoing change. For the cheesemaker, the cheese must be protected from any unwanted contamination, and the best way to ensure its protection is to encourage the rind or outer surface to form a seal. This covering allows the cheese within to develop and interact with the bacteria on the surface. The presence of a natural rind is an indication that the cheese has been made traditionally and by a specialist cheesemaker. As well as an active bacterial rind, some cheesemakers use natural materials such as ash, salt, cloth or oils to form a protective covering.

Factory cheesemaking replaces the need for rind. A variety of methods are used, such as vacuum packaging which draws all the air out of the bag and prevents the risk of bacterial growth. This provides for a safe product but does not allow any development of flavour or maturation.

Specialist cheese goes through a maturation process that requires the control of temperature and humidity. Careful supervision of this process is undertaken and for cheeses that take a long time to mature this is a major investment by the cheesemaker. The cheeses are made in the time-honoured traditional way. Good cheese takes time to make and often months or even years to mature. These efforts result in cheese with full, rich flavours.

SIMON SAYS: THINK OF CHEESE AS SEASONAL AND ENJOY THE DIFFERENT STYLES AT DIFFERENT TIMES OF THE YEAR. IN WINTER BUY AGED CHEESE FROM THE PREVIOUS SPRING RATHER THAN FRESH CHEESE WHEN THE MILK IS NOT AT ITS PEAK.

CHEESE AND ITS MAKERS

FARMHOUSE: Cheese made by hand from milk produced on the farm.

ARTISAN: Specialist cheese made by hand but from milk collected from a number of farms or dairies.

FACTORY OR INDUSTRIAL CHEESE: Cheese made on a large scale using modern technology and bulk milk tankered daily to the factory from dairy farms across a large area.

Cheese can be grouped as follows:

FRESH — uncooked and unripened curd cheeses

WHITE — ripened with a surface white mould rind

WASHED — ripened with a surface rind that is then washed

BLUE — ripened with the addition of blue mould culture

SEMI-HARD — scalded and pressed curd

HARD — cooked pressed curd, with lengthy maturation

PASTEURISED MILK

Most cheese experts agree that the best cheese is made with unpasteurised 'raw' milk. Pasteurisation, they say, robs the milk of some of its flavour and character. In the UK, France, Italy and other cheese-producing European countries, cheese can be made with either pasteurised or unpasteurised milk. But in Australia all cheese, by law, must be made with pasteurised milk and there is a ban on importing cheese made from unpasteurised milk. The exception to this rule is cheese made from cooked raw milk — gruyère and parmesan for example.

SIMON SAYS: FARMHOUSE CHEESE IS MADE FROM THE MILK PRODUCED ON THE FARM. THE CHEESEMAKER CONTROLS THE PROCESS RIGHT FROM THE BEGINNING, INCLUDING THE ALL-IMPORTANT ISSUE OF THE ANIMAL'S HEALTH AND WHAT IT IS FED.

FRESH CURD CHEESE

Fresh curd cheese means the cheese hasn't been ripened (matured) or cooked; these are cheeses to be eaten fresh or as soon as possible after they have been made. Cheeses that fall into this category include fromage frais, fromage blanc, mascarpone, cream cheese and cottage cheese. Fresh goat's and ewe's curd also belong here. Other cheeses that fall into this category are the fresh cheeses marinated in brine or oil such as feta and bocconcini.

Fresh milk is gently heated and a small amount of rennet is added which turns the milk into curds and whey. The curd is gently ladled into moulds and allowed to set. The excess whey drains away through the moulds. The remaining curds, salted or unsalted, are the fresh cheese.

There is a great difference in texture between fresh cheeses: some are smooth and creamy, like fromage blanc, and some are grainy, like

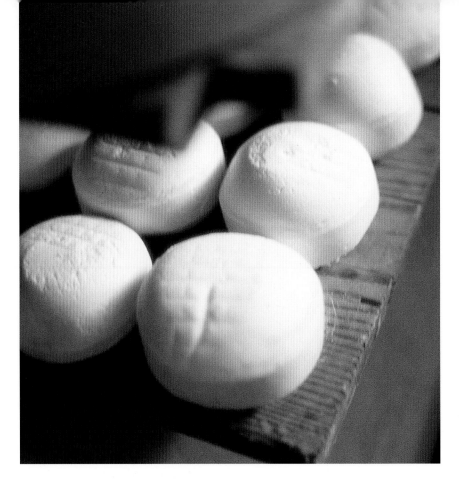

cottage cheese. This is all part of the cheesemaker's art. Soft cheeses need to retain moisture and the delicate curds must be handled carefully to ensure they are not broken and the moisture lost.

Goat's and ewe's milks are particularly suited to soft fresh cheeses and goat's milk is the most popular milk used by specialist cheesemakers for fresh cheeses. Goat's cheese is particularly light and delicious in spring and summer; it can also be eaten at various stages of ripening when its flavour becomes stronger. Well known are the various chèvre style cheeses made in a range of shapes: pyramids, logs and buttons.

To extend the life of these fresh cheeses cheesemakers use various methods to preserve them. Feta has traditionally been preserved in a solution of brine. Fresh goat's cheese is often covered in charcoal or vine ash (*cendré*), which creates a natural rind or protection on the surface of the cheese.

You can make your own version of a fresh cheese by heating 1 litre of full cream milk in a pan over a low heat with 1 teaspoon of salt and 4 teaspoons of lemon juice. Bring slowly to simmering point and simmer for 15 minutes. Add salt to taste. Allow to cool then pour the curds into a muslin cloth and hang over a bowl to drain in a cool place for two or three hours. Refrigerate the resulting fresh-style cheese.

SHORTCUT

Grill a slice of Italian wood-fired bread and top with slices of marinated chèvre feta. Place thinly sliced piquillo pimentos on top and drizzle with extra virgin olive oil. Grind over some black pepper and garnish with a sprig of fresh thyme.

SELECTION AND STORAGE

Fresh cheese should have the light, delicate character of fresh sweet milk. Avoid any cheeses that have a sour smell or musty aroma and a dull or tacky surface. Fresh cheeses are best soon after being made, and spring and autumn are when these cheeses are at their peak.

These cheeses should not be tightly wrapped. Store them in the refrigerator in a container with a lid or on a plate with clingwrap over the top.

TOMATO AND GOAT'S CHEESE TART

Serge Dansereau | Bathers Pavilion
Serves 8

Marinade 4 ripe Roma tomatoes in olive oil, fresh thyme and basil overnight. Cut the tomatoes in half, spoon out the seeds, set on a rack and roast in a preheated oven at 80°C for an hour. Remove the tomato skins.

Sprinkle a blind baked short crust pastry base with fresh thyme, and season with pepper. Slice 250g of mature goat's cheese and spread over the base. Arrange the tomato halves on top of the cheese. Beat 2 eggs with 1/2 cup of cream and 1/2 cup of milk and season lightly with salt and pepper. Pour into the base. Sprinkle with more thyme leaves. Bake in a preheated 180°C oven for 30–35 minutes or until set. Remove from the pan and rest on a rack for 10 minutes. Serve warm with a salad of fresh spinach leaves dressed with extra virgin olive oil and balsamic vinegar.

KERVELLA CHEESE
(Gidgegannup, Western Australia)
Cheesemaker: Gabrielle Kervella

Everyone who hears about Gabrielle Kervella and her goat farm has a similar reaction. There's something heroic about this woman, who is making some of Australia's best cheese from her own herd of goats. Gabrielle raises her goats on her organic farm at Gidgegannup, about 40 minutes north of Perth, Western Australia. She grows and, where necessary, buys organic feed for her goats. The harsh environment means that Gabrielle has to supplement her herd's feed with a variety of organic hay, barley and lupins to produce consistently rich milk. The herd is made up of Anglo Nubian goats, a hardy warm-climate breed, cross-bred with Swiss Saanens, which are known for their milk production. Her breeding program ensures a continuous supply of milk, although the richest cheeses are made in autumn and the more complex cheeses are made in spring.

SALAD OF SPINACH, PEAS, MINT AND WARM GOAT'S CHEESE

Philip Johnson | e'cco
Serves 4

1 baguette
1 or 2 mature goat's cheese logs approximately 5 cm diameter
120g spinach, washed
1 cup fresh peas, podded, blanched and refreshed in ice water
1 cup sugar snap peas, blanched and refreshed in ice water
1/2 cup basil leaves
1/2 cup mint leaves
1/2 cup flat leaf parsley leaves
2 tablespoons sliced green onion
1/2 red onion, thinly sliced
extra virgin olive oil
freshly ground black pepper

Lemon dressing:
50 ml lemon juice
1 teaspoon grain mustard
2 teaspoons thyme leaves
75 ml vegetable oil
75 ml extra virgin olive oil
salt and freshly ground black pepper

TO MAKE THE LEMON DRESSING: Whisk together the lemon juice, mustard and thyme. Add the oils and whisk to combine. Season with salt and pepper.

Slice the baguette into 8 slices on an angle so that the slices are approximately 20 cm x 1.5 cm thick. Slice the cheese logs into 24 slices approximately 5 mm thick.

Toast the baguette slices, top with goat's cheese and warm briefly under a low grill. In a large bowl combine the spinach, peas, basil, mint, parsley and onions. Toss with enough lemon dressing to moisten. Divide the salad between four plates and place two goat's cheese crostini next to each salad, drizzle with extra virgin olive oil and a grind of black pepper.

CROUTE WITH GOAT'S CHEESE AND OVEN-DRIED TOMATOES

Belinda Franks | Belinda Franks Catering

Makes about 20

1 ficelle or thin baguette
extra virgin olive oil
100g goat's cheese

Oven-dried tomatoes:
1 kg Roma tomatoes
salt and freshly ground pepper
caster sugar

TO COOK THE OVEN-DRIED TOMATOES: Cut the tomatoes into 1 cm thick rounds and place in one layer on a baking rack. Sprinkle lightly with the salt, pepper and sugar. Place the rack on an oven tray and bake in a preheated oven at 50°C for approximately three hours. Allow to cool.

Cut the bread into 1 cm thick rounds, lightly brush with the olive oil and place in one layer on an oven tray. Bake in a 180°C preheated oven until lightly toasted. Allow to cool.

Spread the croute with goat's cheese and top with oven-dried tomatoes.

STRETCHED CURD CHEESE

Fresh stretched curd cheeses fit within the category of fresh cheeses, however, they are made differently. After draining, the curds are heated in a vat of hot water and at the right moment they are stretched and pulled. Small pieces of the cheese are removed (mozzare means 'to cut off'), formed into balls, and placed in a cold brine solution. The most popular cheese in this style is bocconcini. Provolone and mozzarella are matured stretched curd cheeses.

SIMON SAYS: BUFFALO MOZZARELLA IS RECOGNISED THROUGHOUT THE WORLD AS THE GREAT ITALIAN MOZ-ZARELLA — IT IS MORE FLAVOURSOME AND HAS A BETTER TEXTURE THAN COW'S MILK MOZZARELLA.

SHORTCUT

Andrew Blake | Blakes

Arrange slices of buffalo mozzarella and vine-ripened tomatoes in a dish. Top with anchovy fillets and drizzle with wine vinegar and extra virgin olive oil.

LASAGNOTTE WITH BUFFALO MOZZARELLA, ARUGULA AND PINE FOREST MUSHROOMS

Sean Moran | Panaroma

Serves 4

400g lasagnotte pasta
2 tablespoons olive oil
4 forest mushrooms (saffron milkcaps or slippery jacks), sliced
salt and freshly ground black pepper
4 cloves garlic, minced
handful sage leaves, chopped
2 tablespoons balsamic vinegar
12 chunks buffalo mozzarella
bunch rocket (arugula)
4 tablespoons parmesan cheese, coarsely grated
1 tablespoon extra virgin olive oil (truffle or chilli oil are good too)

Cook the pasta in boiling salted water.

Heat the olive oil in a large frying pan and add the mushrooms. Turn when golden, season with the salt and pepper and sauté until tender. Add the garlic and sage then deglaze the pan with the vinegar. Remove from the heat. When the pasta is ready, toss it with the mushrooms and add the remaining ingredients. Serve.

WHEY CHEESE

This is cheese made from the whey or the liquid that runs out of the curds. Most whey cheeses are fresh cheeses that are mild and fragile. Ricotta is a well known cheese made from the whey rather than the curd of the milk. It was originally made from ewe's milk, but nowadays it is mostly made from cow's milk. Some ricotta has curd added to the whey, and this is called *ricotta di latte*.

TORTA DI MELANZANE
Anders Ousback | Summit
Serves 4

3 medium eggplants, peeled with a vegetable peeler
salt
1/2 litre olive oil
1 cup mozzarella, grated
1 cup parmesan, grated

Slice the eggplants lengthwise into 1 cm slices. Sprinkle with salt and stand in a colander for about an hour. Wash the salt off the eggplant and pat dry. Shallow fry the slices in olive oil until golden.

In a round pie dish, neatly fan slices of similar sized eggplant over the base. This will become the top of the torta when it is turned out. Scatter half the cheese over this. Add another layer of eggplant. Top with the remaining cheese. Finish with a layer of eggplant. Cook in a preheated 220°C oven for about 45 minutes. As the eggplant cooks it will give off a lot of the oil absorbed when it was being fried which might need to be drained off. Allow the torta to cool enough to turn it out onto a plate. Serve warm or cold cut in wedges. Accompany with a green salad, pesto or freshly made tomato sauce.

TIMBOON
FARMHOUSE CHEESE
(South-west Victoria)
Cheesemaker: Herman Schultz

Herman Schultz started making cheese in 1984 at Timboon, Victoria. A registered bio-dynamic farm, Timboon is committed to farming by natural methods. Schultz's first cheese was a camembert which he still makes by hand today using the organically produced milk from his dairy herd.

SEMI-SOFT CHEESE

These are broken into two categories: white mould and washed rind.

WHITE MOULD

The white mould cheeses that we know best are camembert, brie and triple cream, which are cheeses that are ripened by the introduction of a surface mould rind. The cultivation of the rind using a white mould protects the cheese from contamination and stops the moisture from being lost; it also has a part to play in the development of the flavour and texture of the cheese.

The culture used is *Penicillium candidum*, which gives a pure white mould bloom. The culture is introduced into the milk and after the curds have drained in hoops, the surface is sealed with a light coating of salt, either dry salt or brine. This surface or rind is often sprayed with *Penicillium candidum*. The cheese is then kept at a controlled temperature and humidity while the mould covers the cheese.

Traditionally made cheese matures from the outer rind towards the centre. Ideally this takes up to six weeks. The hard white core that you find in the centre of some white mould cheese is the last part of the curd to be broken down by the maturation process. The cheese is ready to eat when it's soft and buttery throughout, with no chalky centre (except on thicker cheeses such as triple cream, where a chalky heart is characteristic). The rind of a ripe artisan-made white mould cheese may not be perfectly white.

Modern factory-made white mould cheeses are stabilised and do not ripen. This results in reliable cheeses but precludes the ripening and maturation of flavours characteristic of specialist cheese.

WHAT'S THE DIFFERENCE BETWEEN A BRIE AND A CAMEMBERT?

Traditionally a brie is roughly a 2–2.5 kg wheel; a camembert is usually about 250g. The sizes are not chosen arbitrarily: traditional French cheeses ripen perfectly and develop full flavour when made in these sizes. Brie and camembert are made in different regions and the subsequent differing climates, pastures and cultures used to ripen the cheese result in the distinction between the two. Originally bries were made to the south-east of Paris. Authentic French brie is made from raw, unpasteurised milk. The large round shape is important because it exposes a large area to the air which helps ripening. Immature cheese is chalky and acidic but it will become soft and lose the acidic characteristics when properly ripened. Camembert originated in the Normandy region of France. It is identified by a special mark that authenticates it — Véritable Camembert de Normandie (VCN). The cheese is always made to the same size (11 cm) and weight. As it ripens it develops a distinctive flavour and smell that is peculiar to camembert.

MEREDITH DAIRY
(Victoria)
Cheesemakers: Julie and Sandy Cameron

Meredith Dairy, north-west of Geelong in Victoria, is one of Australia's leading producers of ewe's milk and makes ewe's and goat's milk cheese. The enterprise began when sheep farmers Julie and Sandy Cameron met cheesemaker Richard Thomas. The price of sheep had fallen and sheep's milk seemed a good way to add some value to their animals. Sandy Cameron's careful husbandry and use of irrigation on summer pastures has resulted in a consistent milk supply most of the year. These are true farmhouse cheeses with the cheesemaker, Julie Cameron, using only the milk from their farm to produce their cheeses.

SELECTION AND STORAGE

It is easy to identify badly stored or over-ripe white mould cheeses: they are dry and hard, with cracked rinds. They may smell strongly of ammonia or be very runny. These cheeses need to be stored so they remain cool and slightly damp. They should be wrapped in wax-coated paper, which allows the cheese to breathe.

WASHED RIND CHEESE

Washed rind cheese is so-called because during the ripening process the rind is frequently washed in a brine solution with *Brevibacterium linens* and sometimes with beer or wine. The cheese is surface ripened as for white mould cheeses, but the surface or rind development is from bacteria rather than mould. The frequent washing controls the growth of the bacteria and keeps the cheese moist while it matures.

Brevibacterium linens is the most commonly used bacteria. The bacteria on the rind ripens the curds from the outside towards the centre. Washed rind cheese is ripened in an atmosphere of about 95% humidity, which encourages the growth of the bacteria. It develops a complex flavour and the rind becomes sticky with a pungent smell and an orange-red colour (the degree of colour is determined by the washing solution and the bacteria growth).

Most washed rind cheeses are made from cow's milk. Traditionally made cheeses ripen over a period of up to six weeks and develop a rich, soft texture and a pungent aroma.

SIMON SAYS: EXCELLENT EXAMPLES OF WASHED RIND CHEESES ARE KING RIVER GOLD (MILAWA CHEESE COMPANY), HUNTER VALLEY GOLD (HUNTER VALLEY CHEESE COMPANY) AND HEIDI REBLECHON (HEIDI FARM-HOUSE CHEESE).

TALEGGIO (ITALY)

A creamy soft cheese from Lombardy in Italy, Taleggio is matured in the cool microclimates of granite caves. Cheese has been made using the same technique in this region of Italy since the eleventh century.

Taleggio cheese is traditionally square and soft with a thin washed rind. The centre starts out white and chalky and turns smooth and soft as it matures.

SELECTION AND STORAGE

Tasting a washed rind cheese is the best guide to its quality. It should be semi-soft with a complex aroma that should not be ammonic. Washed rind cheeses should be wrapped in waxed paper and stored in a slightly humid spot like the vegetable crisper or a loosely covered container in the refrigerator.

MILAWA CHEESE
COMPANY
(North-east Victoria)
Cheesemaker: David Brown

David and Anne Brown make their cheeses from the milk of cows, goats and ewes in the historic Milawa Butter Factory in the wine region of north-east Victoria. David is one of the leading lights in Australian cheesemaking.
The milk for their cheeses is collected from farms in the surrounding districts. With their encouragement and ongoing support, goat and sheep herds for milking have been established nearby, giving them reliable supplies of milk.
They are best known for their famous washed rind cheese, Milawa gold, and for Milawa blue.

BLUE CHEESE

These are cheeses made by the addition of a blue mould culture, which ripens the cheese from the action of the cultures inside the cheese. This is unlike most cheese where the ripening action is from the rind.

There are two styles of blue cheese, the soft gorgonzola style and the firmer stilton style.

To make the softer style blue cheese, the cheesemaker adds a culture to the curds, being careful to retain the right amount of moisture in the curds, then puts them in a mould to set. The cheese is taken to a cellar, the mould is removed and the cheese is rubbed with salt and left to cure. As it dries out it becomes firm enough to spike.

To make a stilton style blue cheese, the curds are cut to release the moisture, thus creating a drier cheese. Stilton is made with a *Penicillium roqueforti* culture.

The art of blue cheesemaking is to judge the perfect consistency for spiking — if the curd is too soft, the tunnels made by the spikes will collapse into each other. The spikes are like thin skewers and the cheese is spiked from the top and sides depending on the style of cheese. Oxygen gets into the tunnels and activates the culture; this is what forms the blue. As the cheese matures the blue veins spread from the spikes towards the rind.

SELECTION AND STORAGE

An even distribution of blue veins through the cheese indicates it is well made and mature. Because the culture reacts to oxygen the cheese can oxidise quickly. To store the cheese, cut a piece of clingwrap and cover the cut surface of the cheese, pushing the clingwrap against the surface to remove any oxygen. The rind does not need clingwrap. Wrap in wax paper and store in the refrigerator. Blue cheese should be stored on its own or else the flavour and mould could affect other cheeses. Allow the cheese time to reach room temperature before serving.

SIMON SAYS: SOME OF THE BEST BLUE CHEESES MADE IN AUSTRALIA ARE MILAWA BLUE (MILAWA CHEESE COMPANY) AND MEREDITH BLUE (MEREDITH DAIRY).

ROAST PUMPKIN AND MILAWA BLUE RISOTTO

David Brown | Milawa Cheese Company
Serves 4

600–700g pumpkin, peeled and seeds removed
sea salt
extra virgin olive oil
6 cups chicken stock
1 small onion, peeled and finely chopped
2 cups vialone nano rice
Milawa blue cheese
butter
freshly ground black pepper

Cut the pumpkin into 4–5 cm chunks. Place in a baking tin and sprinkle with sea salt. Pour over a little olive oil and roast on the centre shelf of a preheated 200°C oven until the pumpkin is cooked and well browned. Keep the pumpkin warm until you are ready to mix it into the risotto.

Bring the chicken stock to the boil and simmer over a very low heat. Fry the onion in a little olive oil in a heavy pan over low heat until it starts to brown. Add the rice and continue frying for 1–2 minutes, taking care not to burn the onion. Add a ladle of the stock and cook, stirring the rice constantly with a wooden spoon.

Continue to add the stock, stirring constantly as it is absorbed into the rice, for about 18–20 minutes or until the rice is cooked. It should be firm to the bite or al dente but not chalky, and the risotto should be moist and creamy.

Stir in the Milawa blue and a large knob of butter, then carefully fold in the cubes of roasted pumpkin. Season with the black pepper.

Neil Perry | Rockpool

Spread a piece of Meredith blue cheese on a slice of sourdough bread and drizzle with honey.

MISSION FIGS AND MILAWA BLUE GOAT'S CHEESE BAKED IN PASTRY WITH MUSCAT FIG GLAZE

Christine Manfield | Paramount

Serves 6

75g seedless muscatels
200 ml liqueur muscat
250g ripe Mission figs, chopped
125g Milawa blue goat's cheese, crumbled
prepared puff pastry
1 egg
500 ml sugar syrup, made from 250 ml water and 250g sugar
12 black figs, chopped

TO MAKE THE FILLING: Soak the muscatels in the liqueur muscat for at least four hours. Strain the liqueur from the muscatels and set the liqueur aside. In a bowl gently mix together the muscatels, chopped Mission figs and crumbled cheese. Using your hands, form the mixture into six small balls.

TO MAKE THE PASTRIES: Roll out the puff pastry on a floured surface until it is 1 cm thick. Using pastry cutters, cut out six lids 10 cm in diameter and six bases 8 cm in diameter. Leave the pastry rounds refrigerated until ready to assemble.

Lightly beat the egg with a little water. Brush the pastry bases with the egg wash and place a ball of filling on each base. Cover with a pastry lid, press the edges together using your fingers and smooth over. Brush the lids with egg wash and score six arcs around the dome from the centre of the dome down. Refrigerate the pastries for one hour before baking. Bake the pastries in a preheated 180°C oven for 10 minutes until golden. Serve hot with muscat fig glaze.

TO MAKE THE MUSCAT FIG GLAZE: Mix together in a saucepan the liqueur muscat, sugar syrup and black figs. Simmer for 30 minutes on a low heat until reduced. Pour the syrup through a fine mesh sieve and discard the solids.

GORGONZOLA (ITALY)

This is a very ancient cheese dating back many centuries to not long after the time of Christ. It comes from the town of Gorgonzola in Lombardy, just south of the Alps. Gorgonzola is still made in the same locality today with some of the cheese still being matured in mountain caves.

GORGONZOLA PICCANTE is traditionally made in large wheels. It takes three or four months to mature and is more complex with a spicy finish.

GORGONZOLA DOLCE (SWEET) is fast maturing and is not as strong as the traditionally made cheese.

ROQUEFORT (FRANCE)

Roquefort is among the most famous of the French cheeses and is made from unpasteurised ewe's milk. Only a few companies still make this cheese in France. *Penicillium roqueforti* is the mould that is introduced into the cheese. The cheese is matured for at least three months in limestone caves at Cambalou next to the town of Roquefort-sur-Soulzon near the centre of France.

STILTON (UK)

One of England's great cheeses, stilton is the only English cheese that is regionally controlled, i.e. it can be made in only three counties in the east Midlands: Derbyshire, Nottinghamshire and Leicestershire.

CHEDDAR CHEESE

Cheddar is the great semi-hard cheese. It is one of the most popular cheeses made in Australia and New Zealand. Traditionally cheddar is

PYENGANA CHEDDAR
(Tasmania)
Cheesemaker: Jon Healey

Pyengana is one of Australia's oldest specialist cheesemakers who make cheddar in a traditional way using a stirred curd technique. They bind their cheeses in cheesecloth and allow them the time needed to mature. The cheese is made using equipment from the last century.

matured in large wheels. The word 'cheddaring' refers to the way the curd is cheddared or cut into small blocks. The curds are scalded, which makes the curds shrink and expel their moisture. The warm curd is cut into blocks then stacked to press out the whey. As they drain, the lactic acid is evenly distributed through the curd, controlling bacterial growth and texture. After the moisture has been removed and the curds are hooped the surface is rubbed with salt and the cheese wrapped in a cheesecloth and smeared with lard. The cloth allows the cheese to breathe as it matures; this helps it to ripen and gives it flavour. The cheese is turned regularly to maintain an even distribution of moisture, and it is brushed once a week to make sure no bacteria grows on the surface and there are no cracks developing in the cheese. Cheddar is aged for up to two years while its flavour develops.

COOKED & HARD CHEESE

These are cheeses that have the curds preserved by heating and pressing. To make the cheese the curds are scalded so that they shrink, removing their moisture. Then the curds are pressed to remove more moisture. The low moisture content makes a concentrated curd that will mature over time.

Some of the world's great cheeses fall into this category: parmesan, gruyère, tilsit, raclette, emmenthal.

The culture that is added to the milk and the temperature at which the curd is cooked will determine the type of cheese. Cooked cheese has the lowest moisture content of all cheese, and it keeps for the longest time. Cooking gives the cheese a sweet nutty flavour which is caused by the milk caramelising slightly when heated.

Hard cheeses can be matured for two or three or more years. They were originally made in the cold mountain regions of Europe where cheese was only made in the summer months and stored for the winter. These cheeses are among the largest wheels traditionally made, at around 30 kg, which is to allow for a long slow maturation. Traditionally, many farmers joined together to pool their milk so as to make these large cheeses.

PARMESAN

Parmesan is a generic term used to describe a range of Italian 'grana' cheeses, but there is a great deal of difference between them. Parmigiano reggiano is mostly produced in small cheese factories or family run *caselli*. Grana padano is mostly produced in large centres.

PARMIGIANO REGGIANO

Parmigiano reggiano is produced near the towns of Parma and Reggio nell'Emilia in Emilia-Romagna in Italy and dates back to around 700BC. It is made under strict guidelines set down by the Consorzio del Formaggio Parmigiano Reggiano in 1934. The cheese must be made using fresh, unpasteurised cow's milk. When aged for up to 18 months it is called *fresco* (fresh); two-year-old cheeses are called *vecchio* (mature); and three-year-old cheeses are called *stravecchio* (very mature). The cheese rounds are stencilled with the label Parmigiano Reggiano, which is a guarantee of the cheese's authenticity. As it approaches two years of age, reggiano develops a salt-like crunch; this is called enzyme crystallisation and is a sign of proper maturing and quality milk.

GRANA PADANO

Grana padano is made on a bigger scale than parmigiano reggiano and is usually sold when it is less mature. It has been made in the Po Valley of northern Italy since Roman times.

Only cheese that is made using the traditional methods can be called grana padano and parmigiano reggiano.

TO MAKE A GRANA STYLE CHEESE: The cut curds are heated slowly in their whey so that they release their moisture. The curds are cut very finely, about the size of rice grains, to expel the maximum amount of moisture. This grainy mass is put into a cheesecloth and hung to drain then put in a mould and pressed with a heavy weight. Pressing removes more moisture. The rounds of cheese are bathed in brine to start the rind development, then matured for up to two years.

The grana texture is created by cutting the curd finely and cooking at a high temperature — cooking the curd caramelises the lactose, giving it a sweetness, and the finely cut curds give a dense but brittle dryness.

SHORTCUT

Parmesan biscuits

Mix together 125g plain flour and a pinch of cayenne pepper. Rub 60g butter into the flour until it resembles coarse breadcrumbs, add 60g freshly grated parmesan and 1 egg yolk and mix well. You might need a little cold water if the dough is too dry.

Roll the dough out to 1.5 cm thickness and cut into 2.5 cm rounds. Place on a baking sheet and bake in a preheated 150°C oven for 20 minutes.

ROCKET PESTO

Chris Taylor | Fraser's

Blend 3 cloves of garlic, 30g toasted pine nuts, 20g shredded grana padano, a small bunch of rocket leaves and 60 ml of olive oil until well combined. Serve with char-grilled squid or swordfish.

PECORINO

Pecorino is made in a similar way to grana cheeses except that it uses ewe's milk — *pecora* is the Italian word for sheep. The raising of sheep

COW'S MILK:
grana padano and parmigiano reggiano

EWE'S MILK:
pecorino romano and pecorino sardo

has been an important part of Mediterranean life from biblical times and for most of Italy's history pecorino has been one of Italy's prized cheeses. When young, pecorino is a milk-white mild cheese and when mature it is strong and pungent. It is a great table cheese and can be used in much the same way as parmigiano reggiano and grana padano; that is, shaved or grated on pasta or soup. Umbria and Tuscany are reputed to produce the best pecorino.

PASTA SALAD

Alex Herbert

Serves 4 as an appetiser

150g plain flour, unbleached and high in gluten
2 whole 61g eggs
salt and freshly ground pepper
4 tablespoons olive oil
2 tablespoons grana padano cheese, grated
2 red capsicums
4 tablespoons kalamata olives, finely chopped
4 tablespoons Ortiz anchovies, finely julienned
4 tablespoons Italian parsley, roughly chopped
4 tablespoons zucchini, julienned
4 tablespoons grana padano cheese, shaved
4 tablespoons freshly squeezed lemon juice

Place the flour on the work bench in a small mound. Make a well and break the eggs into the well. Lightly beat the eggs, then draw the flour into the eggs. Work with your fingers to amalgamate the flour and eggs into a dough. The dough should be firm, add more flour if it is too wet.

Knead until smooth for about 7 minutes. Rest the dough for at least 15 minutes, then roll out and process through a pasta machine on the spaghetti setting. Cook in boiling salted water until it has lost its raw floury taste, then refresh in cold running water. Drain and season with salt, pepper, olive oil and grated parmesan.

For the salad, grill the red capsicums until their skin starts to bubble and blacken. Place the capsicums in a paper bag until cool. Remove the seeds and peel the skin from the capsicums. Slice into julienne strips. Toss all the remaining ingredients together in a bowl. Add the pasta and leave to soak in all of the flavours for at least 30 minutes before serving.

EMMENTHAL

Emmenthal cheese has a smooth, elastic and pliable texture. This retains more moisture in the cheese. Also these cheeses have eyeholes caused by the starters that have been used in the milk and the heat which activates these organisms producing bubbles of carbon dioxide which become trapped in the cheese.

HEIDI FARMHOUSE
CHEESE
(Exton, Tasmania)
Cheesemaker: Frank Marchand

Frank Marchand is a master cheesemaker from Switzerland. He came to Australia in the 1970s to make cheese for Lactos, one of the pioneering cheesemaking companies of the post-war years. In 1984, with a herd of 100 Friesian cows, Marchand started his own cheesemaking company, Heidi Farm, in northern Tasmania. He set about making the cheeses of his homeland: gruyère, tilsit and raclette.

Heidi Farm has become best known for its gruyère which has won many gold medals. This highly regarded hard-cooked cheese is matured for seven to eight months and ages well for longer. It is one of Australia's largest cheeses at over 30 kg and each one takes about 350 litres of milk to make. The dairy works closely with the seasons and makes cheese from late spring until late autumn.

**SIMON SAYS:
FRANK MARCHAND'S
GRUYERE HAS NO
EQUAL IN AUSTRALIA
AND STANDS UP TO
INTERNATIONAL
COMPARISONS.**

GRUYÈRE

Gruyère was and still is traditionally made in Switzerland and France in the high alpine meadows. This mountain cheese is closely related to emmenthal. The name gruyère is from the mountain pine forests which in days gone by were managed by a special corp called *officiers gruyers*. The pine from these forests was used to build the vats used for cooking the cheese. Gruyère is one of the best eating and cooking cheeses. When cooked it melts evenly and doesn't develop 'strings' so it is perfect for topping gratins and making into sauces.

SELECTION AND STORAGE

Buy these cheeses from the wheel with their natural rinds. The cheese should be moist or waxy but not dry or cracked. The exposed surfaces quickly dry and should be stored wrapped in waxed paper. A good way to store parmesan is wrapped in cheesecloth smeared with olive oil. Place in a plastic bag with plenty of air. Replace the bag regularly if you aren't using the cheese.

MACARONI CHEESE

Damien Pignolet | Bistro Moncur

Serves 4–6

500g orecchiette or maccheroni
55g anchovy fillets
3 teaspoons Keen's dry mustard
100 ml cream
300g mature goat's cheese, crumbled
300g Heidi gruyère cheese, grated
1 cup cooked long grain rice
cayenne pepper

Bechamel sauce:
35g butter
35g flour
1 small onion, peeled

3 cloves
1 bay leaf
1.2 litres milk
salt
3 tomatoes, quartered
120 ml crème frâiche

TO MAKE THE SAUCE: Melt the butter in a saucepan over a gentle heat. Stir in the flour to make a smooth paste or roux and continue stirring over a gentle heat for about three minutes. Put aside to cool for five minutes. Meanwhile, peel the onion and stick the cloves and bay leaf into it. In a saucepan slowly bring the milk almost to the boil with the onion, cloves and bay leaf. Do not allow to boil. Lift out the onion and set aside, discarding the cloves and bay leaf. Pour the hot milk onto the cooled roux, gently heat the mixture and bring back to the boil, stirring all the time. The mixture should thicken to a smooth runny sauce. Add salt if necessary. Add the tomatoes and onion and return to a low simmer. Cover the surface with a greaseproof paper disk and allow to simmer for 30 minutes.

Remove the paper and increase the heat to a gentle boil and reduce a little. Strain into another saucepan and add the crème fraiche. Continue to cook for 10 minutes or until the sauce coats the back of a spoon thickly.

Meanwhile cook the pasta and drain. Chop the anchovy fillets. Mix the mustard to a smooth paste with the cream and add the anchovies. Choose a wide shallow ovenproof dish suitable for serving at the table. Pour a thin layer of the sauce into the bottom of the dish. Spread the pasta evenly over the sauce. Spread the mustard mixture evenly over the pasta. Scatter with the goat's cheese and generously cover it all with sauce. Sprinkle with the grated gruyère cheese and cooked rice and a dusting of cayenne. Bake in a preheated 180°C oven for about 30 minutes or until bubbling hot and well coloured.

SIMON SAYS: ADD SMALL CHUNKS OF GRUYÈRE TO WINTER SOUP JUST BEFORE SERVING. DON'T GRATE IT OR IT WILL MELT TOO QUICKLY; SIMPLY CUT IT INTO PIECES ABOUT THE SIZE OF RASPBERRIES.

THE FROMAGERIE

The role of the *affineur* or *fromager* is to create the perfect climate for cheese. The temperature is kept at 10–14°C, so the cheese is maintained at its best. This is quite a lot warmer than a refrigerator's temperature. Cheesemakers use live cultures and moulds, therefore cheese is a living thing. It is important to create the right conditions for the cheeses to mature while making sure they do not become contaminated with unwanted bacteria. If it is kept too cold the active organisms stop working and the maturation process stops. If it is kept too warm it will sweat and the rind will soften and the texture will change. Humidity is equally important. The storage humidity for most cheeses is ideally about 90–95 per cent. Controlling the temperature and humidity run hand in hand as most modern refrigeration draws moisture out of the air. Humidity must be monitored.

SIMON SAYS: SERVE CHEESE IN THE FRENCH WAY, AFTER THE MAIN COURSE AND BEFORE DESSERT. THE MOMENT YOU INTRODUCE SOMETHING SWEET TO THE PALATE, IT IS CLOSED TO SAVOURY EXPERIENCES.

YOGHURT

Yoghurt is not really cheese — it is thickened by the use of a bacterial starter rather than rennet and unlike cheese none of the liquid is removed. The bacterial starter is composed of *Lactobacillus bulgaricus* and *Streptococcus thermophilus,* which are used in varying ratios. Together they acidify the milk, giving it a slightly sour flavour, and they make the milk more easily digestible. Their balance influences the flavour and texture of the yoghurt. Traditionally made yoghurt is gently heated, the starter added and then allowed to set. Yoghurt can be made from cow's, ewe's and goat's milk.

To make yoghurt at home: Bring almost to the boil 1 litre of milk. Let it cool slightly to 40°C and add two tablespoons of good traditionally made live yoghurt. Pour the milk into a thermos and seal. Set aside

overnight. The yoghurt should slowly set. Store in the refrigerator once it has set.

SHORTCUTS

Serve ewe's milk yoghurt for breakfast with chunks of stone fruit and melon and drizzled with palm syrup, or instead of cream for dessert.

Serve roasted baby lamb racks with a warm salad of chickpeas topped with a spoonful of ewe's milk yoghurt and a drizzle of harissa.

Roast some baby beets, peel and serve drizzled with olive oil and a spoonful of ewe's milk yoghurt.

Marinate chicken pieces overnight in goat's milk yoghurt and fresh coriander before grilling.

CREAM

Cream is the fat contained in milk. In cow's milk the cream naturally rises to the surface but in ewe, goat and buffalo milk it is naturally mixed into the milk. With cow's milk it is much easier to separate the cream out of the milk than it is in other milks. Traditionally cream was separated by skimming the surface of the milk, but modern dairies use centrifugal separators. Cream is divided into:

18–25 PER CENT MILK FAT: Reduced fat or light cream for pouring

35 PER CENT MILK FAT WITH GELATINE ADDED: A good cream for pouring or whipping

35–45 PER CENT MILK FAT: A good cream for cooking or whipping

48–55 PER CENT MILK FAT: Rich double cream ideal for serving with desserts etc.

SOUR CREAM – 35 PER CENT MILK FAT: A sour tangy tasting cream

CREME FRAICHE – 48 PER CENT MILK FAT: A slightly ripened cream

CLOTTED CREAM: Made by scalding cream and leaving it to cool; traditionally it was also slightly ripened but this is no longer done.

MASCARPONE: Cream that is heated, curdled with citric acid, then hung to drain for several days.

HONEY PANNACOTTA
Rita Macali | Luxe
Serves 6

3¹/₂ gelatine leaves
750 ml cream
60g caster sugar
100g honey
270 ml milk

Soak the gelatine leaves in cold water. Combine the cream, sugar and honey in a saucepan and stir over a low heat until it is almost boiling. Remove from the heat.

Remove the gelatine from the water, give it a squeeze and add it to the cream mixture. Bring the cream mixture just to the boil, stirring constantly. Remove from the heat and add the milk. Stir well. Pour the mixture into individual moulds or coffee cups. Refrigerate until set. Serve with dates.

SHORTCUT
Crème Chantilly

Combine 125 ml double cream with 125 ml of thickened cream and add 1 tablespoon of vanilla sugar. Beat by hand with a whisk until the cream doubles in size and forms soft peaks. Keep refrigerated for no more than 1 ¹/₂ hours.

COCONUT MASCARPONE DACQUOISE

Lorraine Godsmark

Serves 4

350g egg whites (approximately 12 eggs)
120g sugar
250g icing sugar, sifted
60g almond meal
225g coconut (half desiccated, half shredded)
icing sugar, extra
500g raspberries

Lightened mascarpone:
3 eggs, separated
100g sugar
500g mascarpone

Raspberry caramel sauce:
300g sugar
210 ml water
250g raspberry purée

TO MAKE THE DACQUOISE: Beat the egg whites until firm peaks form, adding the sugar in three lots. Gently fold in the icing sugar. Combine the almond meal with the coconut and fold into the meringue, being careful not to lose the volume. Pour onto two non-stick baking trays (25 x 37 cm) and spread evenly with a palette knife. Dust with icing sugar and bake in a preheated 170°C oven for 20 minutes or until the top is golden and the centre is soft, a bit like marshmallow. When cool, cut the dacquoise into desired shapes; for instance, triangles or squares.

TO MAKE THE LIGHTENED MASCARPONE: In a mixing bowl, combine the egg yolks and 50g of the sugar with the mascarpone. Whisk to a firm cream. Beat the egg whites with the remaining sugar, until firm peaks form. Gently fold the whites into the mascarpone. Refrigerate until needed.

Make four layers of dacquoise with mascarpone between, topped with raspberries. Refrigerate overnight. Serve with raspberry caramel sauce.

TO MAKE THE RASPBERRY CARAMEL SAUCE: Dissolve all the sugar in 60 ml of the water over a low heat. Wash down the crystals as they form on the side of the pan with a wet pastry brush. Increase the heat and cook to a light caramel colour or until the mixture balls in cold water. Add the remaining water and dissolve the caramel. Allow to cool and add to the raspberry purée.

BUTTER

Butter was developed as a way to preserve milk fat. To make butter, cream is churned until it releases the butterfat. To make half a kilo of butter 10 litres of milk is needed. Most butter is made during the peak milk seasons and stored in frozen blocks.

Butter is sold salted or unsalted, and its flavour depends on when it was made and the quality of the cream used.

Cultured butter (lactic or ripened butter) has a culture of lactic bacteria introduced into the cream. It is then allowed to ripen to develop a slightly acidic flavour before the butter is churned. It is softer than fresh butter and has a more pronounced taste.

BUTTERMILK

This is traditionally the liquid released when butter is churned. Most commercial buttermilks are made from milk and milk powder. Buttermilk has a higher acid content than skim milk and is more easily digested.

SHORTCUT

Pour some garlic oil into hot mashed potatoes with a generous slice of cultured butter and mix well.

ROSTI POTATOES

Philippa Sibley-Cooke | Est Est Est

Peel and grate desirée potatoes, season with salt and freshly ground pepper and rest for 5 minutes. Place the potatoes in a teatowel and squeeze out excess liquid. Fry in hot olive oil and butter until golden. Drain on kitchen paper.

FUNGI

MOST SHOPPERS KNOW EDIBLE mushrooms ONLY AS THE LITTLE WHITE BUTTONS IN THE SUPERMARKETS. BUT THERE ARE LITERALLY HUNDREDS OF thousands OF MUSHROOMS WHICH GROW IN THE WILD THROUGHOUT THE WORLD. EUROPE HAS DINED FOR CENTURIES ON foraged MUSHROOMS. THE EGYPTIANS CONSIDERED MUSHROOMS TO BE THE FOOD OF THE GODS. SOME OF EUROPE'S MOST HIGHLY prized MUSHROOMS ARE CÉPE OR porcini, CHANTERELLE, GIROLLE, MOREL, TROMPETTE AND OF COURSE THE MUCH SOUGHT AFTER truffle. IN FRANCE FORAGING FOR MUSHROOMS IS TAKEN SO SERIOUSLY THAT DURING THE MUSHROOM season, PHARMACISTS OFFER AN IDENTIFICATION SERVICE FOR THE MUSHROOM GATHERER.

In Australia we have hundreds of mushrooms that are native to this country as well as some introduced varieties which can be found in the wild. Only a very few are commonly eaten and great care should be taken when gathering mushrooms.

The most well-known wild mushrooms are the ordinary field mushrooms found in the paddocks in autumn, *agaricus campestris* and *agaricus robinsonii,* with creamy coloured caps and brownish pink gills underneath.

Introduced varieties are the slippery jack or *Suillus luteus* and *Suillus granulatus* which belong to the *Boletus* genus and can also be known as *Boletus granulatus* and *Boletus luteus. Suillus luteus* are spongey under the cap rather than having gills. The cap has a slippery texture and they are usually a dark orange-brown colour. They are

mostly to be found in pine forests. Wipe the slime from the cap and remove the stalks before cooking.

Known as saffron milkcap, the *Lactarius deliciosus* is found mostly in pine forests and is a large fleshy orange-yellow mushroom. It can grow to dinner plate size but the small ones are the best for eating.

Morels, or *Morchella conica*, have a hollow cone shape and the cap is made up of little fissures. These mushrooms are very hard to find and therefore highly prized.

STORAGE

Keep wild mushrooms in the refrigerator but in a paper bag, not in plastic which will make the mushrooms sweat and become slimy. Fresh mushrooms should be prepared and eaten as soon as possible and are best when prepared simply. Mushrooms usually do not need to be washed and most do not need to be peeled; use a damp cloth to wipe off any dirt.

TRUFFLES

Truffles, stemless mushrooms of the genus *Tuber,* are among the most rare and prized foods in the world. They are rare because they have not yet been cultivated. Although truffles have been grown in places like Tasmania, America and New Zealand they remain a wild food. They grow, according to their own whim, underground, in symbiosis with the roots of trees and are hunted rather than harvested, trained pigs and dogs sniffing them out. Truffles are famed because of their marvellous scent and their taste, which many people have extolled but few have been able to describe because truffles taste like nothing else.

There are about thirty varieties of truffle, the best of which fall into two main types:

Black truffles, *Tuber melanosporum,* usually called Périgord truffles, and white truffles, *Tuber magnatum,* also known as Alba or Piedmont truffles.

BLACK TRUFFLES range in size from a walnut to a small fist and are black inside and out. They are harvested between November and March, brushed to remove the soil from their rough, knobbly surface and air-freighted all around the world, often packed in rice. The rice becomes beautifully perfumed, perfect for risotto. So much demand is there for black truffles that even their peelings are sold — these are often used in pâtés. Black truffles are usually lightly cooked or warmed before being eaten, and they're at their best if used simply: with chicken or eggs (a truffle stored in an airtight container with a few eggs will perfume them — scramble the eggs and add truffle shavings).

WHITE TRUFFLES, which are actually putty coloured, are harvested over a very short season in the northern autumn. They are more

BRILLAT-SAVARIN
French gastronome

Truffled turkey has always been popular in France. In 1825, French gastronome Brillat-Savarin wrote, 'I have reason to believe that from the beginning of November to the end of February three hundred truffled turkeys are consumed in Paris every day, or thirty-six thousand in the whole period'. He also had this to say about truffles' reputed aphrodisiac properties: 'The truffle is not a true aphrodisiac; but in certain circumstances it can make women more affectionate and men more attentive'. We do know that the production of truffles has been in decline since the beginning of the century. This may be because of the decline in the number of oak trees which play host to the truffle or the changes towards urban lifestyles.

strongly perfumed than black truffles. They are eaten raw, shaved over risotto, or added to a simple salad or plain pasta dish. The famous truffle dish of Piedmont is a fondue made with the local fontina cheese and generously covered with fine shavings of white truffles.

Summer truffles—black on the outside, white within—are flavourless and do not compare.

Fresh truffles can't be kept long, but they are also available canned. When you buy canned truffles, make sure they're labelled *premier cuisson* (first cooking) to get the best quality.

THE TRUFFLE MARKET
There are about ten truffle markets still operating in France and a truffle hunter can still gather around 20–25 kg of truffles depending on the year. There is a great air of intrigue at the markets because the truffle hunters do not wish to divulge the locality of their truffle finds or the price that is paid for them. Brokers operate at the markets making their offers on pieces of paper which are shown to the sellers. If they accept the offer they then take the paper. The famous Périgord region, home of the Périgord truffle, produces only about 2 tonnes of the 30 or so tonnes of 'Périgord truffles' produced in France.

TRUFFLED CHICKEN COOKED IN A BAG
Neil Perry | Rockpool
Serves 2

1 x 1.8 kg corn-fed chicken
120g unsalted butter
1 small leek, cut into julienne
1/2 small onion, finely sliced
1 clove garlic
1 small carrot, peeled and cut into julienne
sea salt and freshly ground pepper
50 to 100g fresh truffles, depending how far your love goes
60 ml chicken stock

Basmati rice:
1 cup basmati rice
3 tablespoons olive oil
1/2 onion, diced
sea salt
1 3/4 cups chicken stock
truffle peelings or peelings and 10g truffles, cut into julienne

Place the chicken on a board and remove the winglets. Cut off the neck and remove the wishbone — it makes carving easier. Take the fatty glands out of the cavity and rinse the chicken. Pat dry with kitchen paper.

Melt half the butter in a heavy-based saucepan and gently stew the leek, onion, garlic and carrot with a pinch of salt until soft. Remove from the heat. Stuff the chicken with the vegetables. Peel the truffles and reserve the skin. Slice into fine rounds.

Bring some water to the boil in a steamer. Put your finger under the skin of the breast to loosen the skin from the flesh, and gently work your way up to the thighs and drumsticks. Carefully slide slice after slice of truffle up under the skin, stuffing the drumsticks and working your way back to the breast. The chicken should look black, with bits of white flesh in-between. Rub the rest of the butter over the chicken, season with salt and pepper, and place in a large oven bag. Pour over the stock and seal the bag with a twist. Place in the steamer and steam for 1 1/2 hours. Remove from the steamer and allow to sit for 10 minutes.

TO PREPARE THE BASMATI RICE: Sauté the rice in the oil in a little pot with a tight-fitting lid. Add the onion and fry until it is coated. Add the sea salt, stock, truffles and bring to the boil. Put the lid on and cook on a low heat for 15 minutes. Place a pastry ring or wok ring under the pot, and turn the heat down as low as it will go. Heat for a further 10 minutes. Take to the table and serve with the truffled chicken.

It is best to open the bag at the table so that your guest can savour the aroma. Remove the chicken from the bag. Cut off the leg and remove the breast. Place a leg and breast on each plate. Take the aromatic vegetables out of the cavity and place on the plate. Spoon the cooking juices over the chicken, and serve with the truffled basmati rice and a salad.

GNOCCHI WITH BLACK TRUFFLES, BURNT BUTTER AND PARMESAN

Stefano Manfredi | bel mondo

Serves 6–8 as a first course

1 1/2 kg desirée potatoes
plain flour
2 egg yolks
salt
150g parmesan, grated
1/2 teaspoon nutmeg, grated
butter
fresh black truffles, thinly shaved

Cook the whole, unpeeled potatoes in a little water with the lid on the pot, which will virtually steam the potatoes and limits the water they retain. Choose potatoes that do not retain a lot of moisture, such as desirée or pink eye. Old potatoes are generally better than new potatoes. While still hot, peel the potatoes and mash them with a potato masher. Do not put them in a blender. Set aside to cool.

On a work bench, make a well in the centre of the mound of potato. Add a handful of flour, the egg yolks, a good pinch of salt, a small handful of parmesan and the grated nutmeg. Fold the mixture together continually toward the centre, gradually adding more flour if necessary; remember that the more flour that is added, the firmer the gnocchi will be. The mixture should be soft, smooth and slightly sticky. Once the mixture has come together, allow it to rest for five minutes. Shape the gnocchi into sausage-like rolls about as thick as your thumb, then cut into 14 mm lengths.

Poach the gnocchi in plenty of salted boiling water (not furiously boiling) until they float to the surface. Lift them out with a slotted spoon and place on plates. Meanwhile, place the butter in a small pot over a high heat until it has gone a nut brown colour. Turn off the heat, sprinkle the gnocchi with parmesan, sprinkle with the shaved truffles and spoon the sizzling butter over the top. Serve immediately.

SIMON SAYS: THE FOODS THAT REALLY GO WELL WITH TRUFFLES ARE EGGS, POTATOES AND PASTA.

PORCINI

These wild mushrooms are known in France by the name cèpes, and in Italy by the name porcini. At the end of August until November, in the woods of the Gironde, the forests to the south of Bordeaux and the chestnut forests of Piedmont in Italy, the arrival of these brown-capped, fat-stemmed cèpes is awaited eagerly. They are well camou-flaged and difficult to detect among the oak and chestnut leaves on the forest floor. These spongy mushrooms are known botanically as *Boletus edulis*. The Italian name of porcini is taken from the Italian word for pigs who forage in the forests and like to eat them. The Italians regard porcini as the king of mushrooms.

The mushrooms are gathered from the forest floors and either sold fresh through the markets or dried. In the traditional method used for drying, the mushrooms are sliced, threaded onto string and hung up to dry in the sun. Dried porcini are an ingredient on their own. As they dry the flavour is concentrated and this gives a unique aromatic addition to dishes.

To use dried porcini they need to be soaked in warm water for 30 minutes and then you can add them to your dish; they only take 15–20 minutes to become tender. Make sure you keep the liquid they were soaked in, and add it to soups and stews, or if you're making a porcini risotto, use it as part of the stock.

SHORTCUTS

Grind porcini and sea salt together in a food processor and sprinkle over steak and vegetables.

Crush porcini to a fine powder with a mortar and pestle and add it to a veal ragout to add a delicious earthy flavour — or sprinkle it over fish or chicken prior to grilling or barbecueing.

PORCINI RISOTTO

Raymond Capaldi
Serves 6

2 tablespoons extra virgin olive oil
2 tablespoons unsalted butter
1 small onion, peeled and finely chopped
20g porcini mushrooms, soaked in a little warm water for 15 minutes
250g button mushrooms, sliced
500g vialone nano rice
1 litre boiling beef stock
sea salt and freshly ground black pepper
2 tablespoons grated parmesan
unsalted butter, extra
1 tablespoon flat leaf parsley, chopped

Heat the oil and half the butter in a pan, add the onion and cook over low heat until soft but not brown. Drain the porcini, reserving their soaking liquid, and chop coarsely. Add to the pan, stir for a few seconds and add a quarter of the button mushrooms. Sauté until they begin to brown, then add the rice and stir until it becomes opaque.

Add the reserved porcini liquid and a ladleful of the boiling stock. Stir continuously while adding the stock, a ladleful at a time, allowing the rice to absorb the stock before each new addition. Cook in this way until the rice has absorbed all the stock and is tender. Add the salt and pepper, remove the pan from the heat and stir in the remaining butter and the parmesan. Allow to rest while you sauté the remaining button mushrooms in the extra butter. Stir them into the risotto with the parsley and serve immediately.

GRAINS & PULSES

PULSES AND grains CAN PROVIDE ALL THE CARBOHYDRATE HUMANS NEED

AND THE COMBINATION OF THESE STAPLES HAVE sustained HUMANKIND

THROUGHOUT THE WORLD. IN NORTH AFRICA THERE IS COUSCOUS; IN ASIA, RICE,

noodles AND SOY BEANS; IN ITALY PASTA AND RISOTTO; IN INDIA, dhal,

BEANS AND RICE; IN THE MIDDLE EAST, RICE AND CHICKPEAS — THESE STAPLES

OF COOKING HAVE INEXTRICABLY BEEN woven INTO THE CULTURAL FABRIC

OF CIVILISATIONS THROUGHOUT HISTORY. CHICKPEAS AND ALL KINDS OF

beans, LENTILS AND PEAS WERE PART OF THE PEASANT FOODS OF THE

MEDITERRANEAN, AND ARE STILL USED TODAY IN SALADS, STEWS AND SOUPS. THEY

ARE A RICH SOURCE OF NUTRIENTS AND ARE EXCEPTIONALLY healthy. CORN,

RICE AND wheat ARE ALSO STAPLES AND HARDLY A MEAL GOES BY WITHOUT

ONE OR THE OTHER BEING SERVED.

PASTA & NOODLES

Legend has it that Marco Polo brought the secret of pasta back to Italy from China in the thirteenth century, but both the Italians and the Chinese were familiar with it long before his time. It is a staple of so many cultures that no one knows who invented it. The dividing line between pasta and noodles is extremely fine. Pasta is usually made from a basic mixture of hard wheat flour or semolina and water. Eggs and vegetable flavourings are sometimes added. Noodles are made from a variety of flours including wheat, buckwheat, soya bean, mung bean and rice, plus water and sometimes eggs. Increasingly, Asian ingredients are being tossed through pasta, while noodles are often used for Western dishes.

PASTA

Quality pasta is made from durum wheat which is strong and hard and contains a high proportion of gluten, which makes the dough elastic. The best pasta is labelled *pasta di semola di grano duro*, which translates to 'pasta of hard wheat flour'. It holds its shape and texture when cooked.

The best pasta has a dull finish and tiny abrasions in the texture. Artisan-made pasta uses the traditional method of extruding through bronze dies, resulting in a rough surface on the pasta — the advantage of this is that the porous surface traps and holds the sauce. And instead of drying the extruded dough quickly at high temperatures, artisans use the classic method of slow drying at low temperatures, paying special attention to air circulation and levels of humidity. This process can take as long as three days to complete for short pasta, less time for long pasta. Shiny, smooth pasta is extruded through stainless steel or teflon dies which give it a smooth, even surface, and it is then heat dried.

COOKING PASTA

The most important thing to know about cooking pasta is to use lots of water. Never try to cook pasta in a small pan.

Bring the water to the boil and add sea salt — the amount will depend on the saltiness of the sauce you are serving.

When the water is rapidly boiling add the pasta, making sure it is completely covered with water; wait until the water returns to the boil and then give it a stir. Boil rapidly until al dente.

WHAT IS AL DENTE?

Al dente means 'to the tooth' or a firmness to the tooth. The only way to test pasta is to taste it; take no notice of how long it says to cook it on the pack, use your own judgment.

Start tasting soon after you have added the pasta to boiling water and keep tasting until it's cooked through but still firm to the bite — a toothy tenderness, it's often called. Drain it and mix it immediately with sauce. If you leave it standing before tossing with sauce, it will stick together.

WHICH PASTA WITH WHICH SAUCE?

By choosing the right pasta or shape for the sauce you are making, the sauce will coat and cling to each pasta, so you will have a better result. **LONG PASTA** such as spaghetti needs a sauce that will cling to it; a thick but smooth sauce such as a tomato sauce.

LATINI PASTA
Osimo, Adriatic Coast, Italy

Carlo and Carla Latini are wheat growers who have their own pastificio or pasta factory. They grow the durum wheat they use in their pasta, which means they control its quality right from the start. Milling the durum wheat and making the pasta immediately helps it retain the wheat flavour. They employ traditional slow-drying methods and the same bronze extruding machines that have been used for generations. These machines give the pasta its characteristic rough texture. The Latini company makes pasta in such limited quantities that it numbers each 500g pack. It also makes a limited quantity of pasta from a single variety of durum wheat called Senatore Cappelli, it is a very old, low-yielding grain, which was widely grown 100 years ago and is one of the world's great durum wheat varieties.

Benedetto Cavalieri in Italy's Puglia is another passionate artisan. Many of the pasta shapes he produces, such as orecchiette, are typically only produced in southern Italy.

HOLLOW-CUT PASTA, SHELLS AND SPIRALS will trap sauce in their hollows, so these are best with sauces that contain chunks of meat or seafood.

GROOVED OR RIDGED PASTA perfectly traps thin sauces.

FLAT PASTA such as tagliatelle is good with creamy sauces.

RISONI and other small grain-shaped pasta is best in soup.

PAPPARDELLE is ideal with robust, chunky sauces.

SPAGHETTI CON MARINATA DI ERBE

Lucio Galletto | Lucio's
Serves 4

3 ripe tomatoes
1/3 cup of mixed fresh herbs (basil, oregano, thyme, parsley, marjoram etc.)
2 anchovies, chopped
1/2 cup black olives, pitted
1/2 cup green olives, pitted
1 teaspoon capers, chopped
2 cloves garlic, finely chopped
6 tablespoons olive oil
1 teaspoon red wine vinegar
300g spaghetti

Peel, seed and dice the tomatoes. Chop the herbs. In a large bowl, place all the ingredients with the oil and vinegar, mix well and let it rest for about an hour. Cook the spaghetti until al dente. Drain and add to the herb mixture. Toss quickly and serve immediately.

There are literally hundreds of pasta shapes and more are being invented every day.

BUCATINI: Thick, hollow spaghetti.

CONCHIGLIE: Resembles sea shells.

FARFALLE: This means butterflies; the pasta looks like little bows.

FUSILLI: Corkscrew shaped spaghetti.

LINGUINE: Flat pasta like an Asian noodle.

MACCHERONCINI: Small, stubby, hollow macaroni.

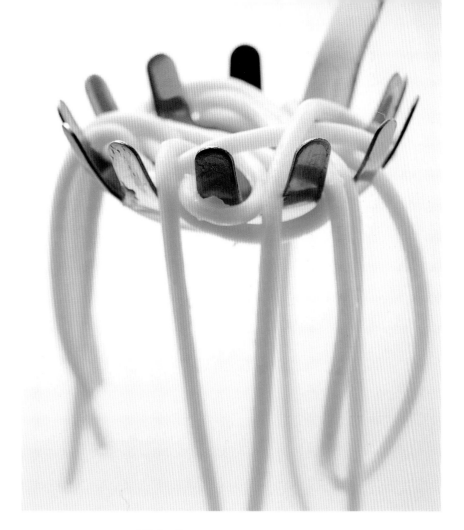

PAPPARDELLE: Wide flat pasta.

PASTINA: Miniature pasta like anelli, acini, risoni etc.

PENNE: Hollow cut pasta shaped like a quill.

RIGATONI: Stubby, hollow, slightly curved and ridged pasta.

RUOTE DI CARRO: Cart wheel shapes.

ZITI: Short tubular shape like rigatoni, except narrower and not ridged.

FETTUCCINE WITH SCALLOPS

Prue Hill

Serves 4

Peel, seed and roughly dice egg tomatoes and set aside. Roast and crush half a teaspoon of coriander seeds and mix with the zest and juice of a lemon, a handful of chopped fresh coriander, some extra virgin olive oil, pepper and salt. Stir in lightly fried scallops and mix with freshly cooked fettuccine. Top with the diced tomatoes.

LINGUINE WITH PRAWNS

Liam Tomlin | Banc

Sauté peeled green prawns in extra virgin olive oil until cooked.
Roast a yellow and a red capsicum, peel and dice. Add the capsicum
to freshly cooked linguine with small black olives, roughly chopped
flat leaf parsley, salt, pepper and lemon-infused oil. Serve the
prawns on top.

SPAGHETTINI COOKED 'EN PAPILLOTE' WITH ARUGULA, SHIITAKE MUSHROOMS AND CHILLI OIL

Dietmar Sawyere | Forty One

Serves 6

silicone paper
200g cooked spaghettini
30 ml chilli oil
sea salt
white pepper
200g fresh shiitake mushrooms, sliced
120g arugula
100g enoki mushrooms
red chillies, thinly sliced
lemon juice
60g garlic butter

Cut six large heart shapes out of silicone paper. Toss the spaghettini
with the chilli oil and season well with salt and pepper. Place some
on one side of each heart shape. Place the shiitake mushrooms,
arugula leaves, enoki mushrooms and two slices of red chilli on the
pasta. Sprinkle with lemon juice and place 10g of garlic butter on
top of each.

Fold over the other side of the heart shape, and starting at the wide
end, fold the edges over, sealing the parcel closed. Ensure the
parcels are tightly closed. Bake in a preheated 200°C oven for 5–6
minutes. Serve the parcels unopened with a wedge of lemon.

NOODLES

In Asia noodles are enjoyed at every meal and for snacks in between meals. Each Asian country has its own favourite noodles and particular ways to serve them. The key to describing noodles is the grain that is used to make them.

WHEAT

WHEAT NOODLES AND EGG NOODLES are made of soft wheat flour and water. If egg has been used they are labelled as egg noodles. They are sold fresh or dried and are used in stir fries or soups or served instead of rice with main dishes. Flat noodles are usually used in soups and round ones for stir-fries.

SOMEN AND UDON are Japanese noodles made of wheat flour and used in soup or served with main dishes.

RICE

RICE VERMICELLI look like fine skeins of white wire and can be added to soup, such as laksa, or fried or steamed. They should be soaked before using except when steamed.

RICE NOODLES are made from ground rice that is steamed and cut into ribbons, and are used in soups, stir fries and served with a sauce.

RICE STICK NOODLES are made of rice and tapioca flours and dried. They are used in soups and stir fries and need to be soaked then cooked for a moment in hot water.

BUCKWHEAT

SOBA NOODLES are a Japanese noodle that are cooked and used in soup or eaten with other ingredients.

MUNG BEAN (WHICH IS NOT A GRAIN)

CELLOPHANE NOODLES are made from ground mung beans.

They are very fine, white dried noodles. Soak in warm water for five minutes until they are soft before using then add to soups or braised dishes. They can also be deep fried without soaking.

KEN HOM'S SINGAPORE NOODLES

Ken Hom

Serves 4–6

225g thin dried rice noodles
50g Chinese black mushrooms
175g frozen small sweet peas
4 eggs, beaten
1 tablespoon Chinese sesame oil
1 teaspoon salt

1/2 teaspoon freshly ground white pepper

3 tablespoons groundnut or peanut oil

1 1/2 tablespoons garlic, finely chopped

1 tablespoon fresh ginger, finely chopped

6 fresh red or green chillies, de-seeded and finely shredded

6 whole fresh water chestnuts

100g Chinese barbecue pork or cooked ham, finely shredded

3 spring onions, finely shredded

100g small cooked prawns, shelled

fresh coriander leaves

Curry sauce:

2 tablespoons light soy sauce

3 tablespoons Indian Madras curry paste or powder

2 tablespoons Shaoxing rice wine or dry sherry

1 tablespoon sugar

1 teaspoon salt

1 teaspoon freshly ground black pepper

250 ml coconut milk

175 ml chicken stock

Soak the rice noodles in a bowl of warm water for 25 minutes. Then drain in a colander or sieve. Set them aside until you are ready to use them. Soak the mushrooms in warm water for 20 minutes, then drain them and squeeze out the excess liquid. Remove and discard the stems and finely shred the caps into thin strips. Put the peas in a small bowl and let them thaw. Combine the eggs with the sesame oil, salt and pepper and set aside.

Heat a wok or large frying pan over high heat until it is hot. Add the oil, and when it is very hot and slightly smoking, add the garlic, ginger and chilli and stir-fry the mixture for 30 seconds. Then add the water chestnuts, mushrooms, pork or ham, and spring onions for 1 minute. Then the rice noodles, prawns, peas, and continue to stir-fry for 2 minutes. Now add all the sauce ingredients and continue to cook over high heat for another 5 minutes or until most of the liquid has evaporated. Lastly add the egg mixture over the noodles and stir-fry constantly until the egg has set.

Turn the noodles onto a large platter, sprinkle with the coriander leaves and serve at once.

For a vegetarian version, replace stock with extra coconut milk.

COUSCOUS

A staple of North African cuisine, couscous is semolina rolled into tiny pellets and coated in semolina flour. It is traditionally cooked in a *couscoussière*, a pot with a perforated colander-like bowl that sits on top. Meat or chicken with vegetables and chickpeas simmer in the bottom part of the pot and the couscous steams above it. A muslin-lined colander placed over a pot will do almost as well. Couscous also comes pre-cooked, as 'instant' couscous; all you have to do is add hot liquid. Couscous makes a wonderful background to meat or vegetable stews. Once it is cooked, fluff with a fork before serving.

LAMB TAGINE WITH ARTICHOKES, LEMON AND OLIVES

Meera Freeman
Serves 4

1.5 kg lamb shoulder, cut into large chunks
1/4 cup olive oil
2 cloves garlic, peeled and crushed
salt
1/4 teaspoon freshly ground black pepper
1 1/2 teaspoons ground ginger
2 pinches saffron threads
1/4 teaspoon turmeric
1/4 cup grated onion
1 cup water
8–10 fresh small artichokes
2 preserved lemons, rinsed and pulp removed
3 tablespoons lemon juice
1/2 cup Arbequina olives

In a saucepan, toss the lamb chunks with the oil, garlic, salt and pepper, spices and onion. Cover with water and bring to the boil. Reduce the heat, cover and simmer over moderate heat for 1 1/2 hours, turning the pieces of meat often in the sauce and adding water whenever necessary.

In the meantime, prepare the artichokes by removing the outside leaves and trimming the bases. Place in acidulated water to keep from blackening. Rinse and drain before using.

Put the artichokes in a casserole with the meat and simmer for 15–20 minutes until tender. Add the rinsed preserved lemon, cut into strips and cook for another 10 minutes. Sprinkle with the lemon juice and the olives and cook a few minutes together. Serve with couscous.

SHORTCUT

Mix some sliced preserved lemon rind and a handful of raisins through cooked instant couscous and serve with chicken casserole.

CORN

Corn has an extraordinary range of uses throughout the world. It is particularly popular in the Americas where it is used to make oil, syrup, corn starch, flour, chips, popcorn, tacos, bread, cakes and lots more. It is the only cereal crop that is native to the Americas, originating in Mexico. But within 50 years of Columbus bringing corn back to Spain it was grown all over Europe.

POLENTA

One of the most famous dishes of the Piedmont region of Italy, polenta is made from coarsely ground cornmeal. This is a peasant dish that is a little like porridge. The cornmeal is made from a yellow corn that has very hard hulls. Traditionally peasants harvested corn in autumn and air dried the cobs in their husks over winter. In the spring they milled the kernels into a stone-ground meal. The very best cornmeal made today is stone-ground and made from naturally dried corn kernels.

Dry polenta is added to boiling salted water or stock and stirred (using a long-handled spoon, because it can splatter as it cooks) until it is thick and smooth, and butter and parmesan are added for extra flavour. It requires patience and a strong arm for stirring. It can be eaten as it is, or poured into a baking dish, cooled until set, cut into squares and grilled or fried. Serve it with grilled or baked vegetables or roasted meats. It is delicious used as the base for roasted quail or other game birds, absorbing and being flavoured by their juices. Polenta complements many ingredients: olives, sun-dried tomatoes, mozzarella or other cheeses, and a really elegant version of this peasant dish can be made with porcini or truffles. Buckwheat polenta is rustic in taste with a big flavour that goes well with game birds, and is also a favourite with vegetarians.

POLENTA
Serves 4

1 1/2 litres water
1 teaspoon salt
300g polenta

Bring the water to the boil in a large, heavy-bottomed saucepan. Add a large pinch of salt, then turn the heat down to medium low so the water is at a steady simmer. Add the polenta in a thin stream, stirring all the time. Continue stirring for about 20 minutes after all the polenta has been added. When cooked the polenta will tear away from the sides of the pot as it is stirred. Serve immediately or pour the polenta into a flat dish or onto a wooden board. Allow to cool enough to slice.

SHORTCUT

Cook polenta in chicken stock with crushed garlic cloves. Pour into a flat dish and allow to cool. Cut into slices, brush with olive oil and char-grill. Sauté two or three different types of fresh mushroom in olive oil and sliced garlic. Add a little chicken stock and, when they are ready, sprinkle with roughly chopped flat leaf parsley. Spoon the mushrooms over the polenta.

BRAISED BRISKET WITH OLIVES ON SOFT POLENTA

Anthony Musarra | Lucciola
Serves 6–8

olive oil
2 large brown onions, peeled and chopped
8 cloves garlic, peeled
2 carrots, peeled and chopped
2 sticks celery, chopped
1 tablespoon tomato paste
500 ml dry red wine
250 ml balsamic vinegar
4 litres beef stock
1 cinnamon stick
2 sprigs oregano
2 sprigs rosemary
1 tablespoon black peppercorns
2 bay leaves
1 x 2 kg beef brisket, trimmed of excess fat
salt and freshly ground pepper
150g Sommariva Ligurian olives, pitted
Soft polenta (recipe follows)

Place a little olive oil in a large wide pot and heat. Add the onions, garlic, carrots and celery and cook until well coloured. Add the tomato paste and cook over a high heat for 2 minutes before adding the wine and vinegar. Cook for 3–4 minutes, then add the beef stock, cinnamon stick, oregano, rosemary, peppercorns and bay leaves. Bring to the boil and simmer for 5 minutes.

Season the brisket with salt and pepper. Brown well on all sides in a hot pan with a little olive oil, or on a hot, flat grill. Place in a deep baking dish and pour the stock mix over. Cover with foil, then place in a preheated 180°C oven for approximately 4–5 hours, or until the meat is extremely soft. Keep hot in the liquid.

To serve, place a spoonful of polenta into deep bowls. Remove the brisket from the liquid. Cut into thick slices, then place on top of the polenta. Serve with some of the olives and the braising liquid. Steamed green vegetables such as spinach or baby bok choy are a good accompaniment to this dish.

SOFT POLENTA

Anthony Musarra | Lucciola
Serves 6–8

700 ml water
200 ml milk
250g polenta
2 tablespoons grana, grated
1 tablespoon unsalted butter
1 clove garlic, peeled and crushed
salt and freshly ground pepper

Bring the water and milk to the boil then 'rain in' the polenta, whisking constantly. Continue to cook, stirring all the time, for approximately 35–40 minutes. Remove from the heat and add the grana, butter and garlic. Season with salt and pepper. Keep hot.

SIMON SAYS: CUT POLENTA INTO THICK SLICES, BRUSH WITH OLIVE OIL AND BARBECUE UNTIL CRISP ON THE OUTSIDE. WHILE STILL HOT, PUT THIN SLICES OF GORGONZOLA ON TOP AND ALLOW TO MELT.

RICE

There are thousands of different varieties of rice grown throughout the world, the majority in Asia, where the freshness, texture, colour and fragrance are all important in determining the quality and end use of the different rices. Rice has been a regular part of the Asian diet for about 3000 years.

It is believed that the origins of rice are in Asia and from there the Persians and Mesopotamians came into contact with it. It spread throughout the Ottoman Empire where it became a staple and eventually reached Italy and Spain. It became one of the distinctive ingredients of the Mediterranean region and is part of the great tradition of peasant cookery in a single pan, which has produced two of the classic rice dishes: risotto and paella. Many different varieties grow in

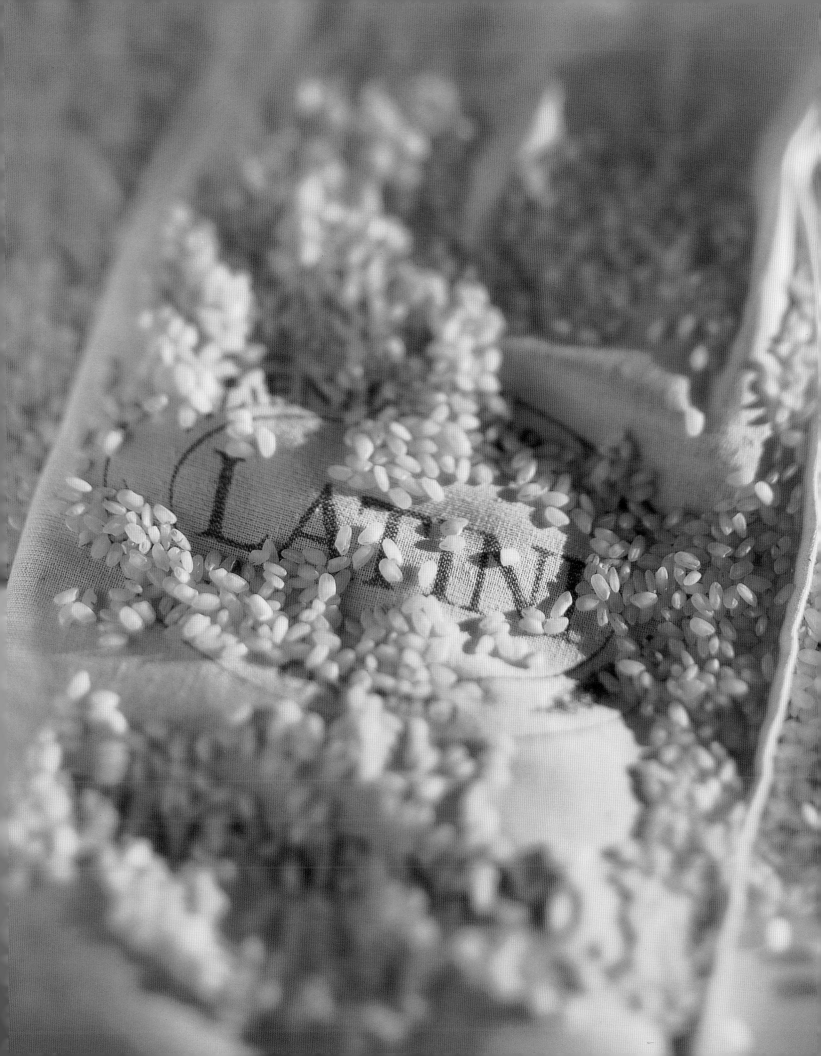

the marshland areas of the Mediterranean, the most prolific being the Po delta in Italy. In Europe it wasn't much known before the thirteenth century and was initially regarded as a spice—which seems incongruous in view of its subtle flavours.

Rice can be divided into three categories: long grain, medium grain and short grain.

LONG GRAIN RICE: When cooked the grains remain separate and the rice looks light and fluffy. Long grain rice is the most popular rice for cooking in China. Basmati, patna, jasmine or Thai fragrant rice are all long grain.

SHORT AND MEDIUM GRAIN RICE: These are rounder grains than long grain rice and the grains cling together. Short grain rices are used in Spain for paella dishes, in Italy for risotto, Japan for sushi, China for sticky rice and England for rice pudding. Arborio, carnaroli and vialone are varieties used to make risotto.

RISOTTO

Not surprisingly, the best rice for risotto is grown in northern Italy, the home of risotto, where it has been grown on a relatively small scale since the sixteenth century. Risotto rice is round grained with an opaque pearly centre; its unique quality is its ability to absorb up to twice its own grain weight of liquid over a long cooking time without losing its shape. There are four categories of risotto rice: *super-fini, semi-fini, fini* and *arborio*. These classifications have nothing to do with the quality of the rice; they describe the size of the grain, from super-fini (largest) to arborio (smallest).

Vialone nano and carnaroli are regarded as the very best varieties of risotto rices. Vialone nano rice has an extraordinary capacity to absorb liquid without losing its shape. The larger-grained carnaroli rice absorbs less liquid and remains slightly more al dente.

SEASONING A PAELLA PAN

A paella pan should be kept just for making paella. And, like an omelette pan or a wok, it should be seasoned before use. Wash the paella pan thoroughly and dry it with kitchen paper. Put it over high heat and pour in a little olive oil. Move the pan around until the oil covers the entire surface. Add some sliced onions, reduce the heat and simmer until the onions are brown. Remove the pan from the heat and leave until the oil and onions are cold. Remove and discard the oil and onions, wash the pan again and dry it thoroughly. Rub the surface of the paella pan with kitchen paper dipped in olive oil. The pan is now ready to be stored. Wash and dry the pan before you re-use it, and always give it a light coating of olive oil before storing to avoid rusting.

When making risotto, remember that it must be creamy, not dry; it should have the consistency of a thick soup. Serve risotto the minute it is cooked.

SIMON SAYS: GRAINS OF UNIFORM SIZE ARE VERY IMPORTANT IN MAKING THE PERFECT, EVENLY COOKED RISOTTO.

PAELLA

Paella should be cooked in a traditional two-handled paella pan — wide and shallow with a flat base — and brought to the table in the same dish. It is eaten with a spoon. Although there are countless variations of paella it always contains rice, saffron and olive oil and, usually, chicken, pork and shellfish.

CALASPARRA RICE
(Murcia, Spain)

Calasparra is the short grain rice used in paella, and the best of it grows in the province of Murcia on the east coast of Spain. It is grown on ancient terraces, fed by the waters of the Segura and Mundo rivers. Calasparra carries the DO (Denominación de Origen) stamp, the official government stamp ensuring the highest quality and guaranteeing that it comes from a specific region.

RISOTTO ALLA MILANESE

Meera Freeman
Serves 4

80g butter
1 piece of beef marrow the size of an egg, chopped
1 shallot, finely chopped
500g vialone nano rice
1 litre hot beef stock
1 teaspoon saffron threads
sea salt and freshly ground pepper
1/2 cup parmigiano reggiano, grated

Place half the butter and the beef marrow in a pan with the shallot and sauté until the shallot is soft but not brown. Add the rice, turning it until it becomes opaque. Stirring continuously add the stock, a ladleful at a time, allowing the rice to absorb it and dry out before adding the next ladleful. When the rice is half cooked, add the saffron to the remaining stock and continue to add it to the rice as before until the rice is tender. Taste for salt and pepper. Add the rest of the butter and the grated cheese and serve immediately.

ANICA PANIC'S SULTIJAS (RICE PUDDING)

Joan Campbell
Serves 4–6

1/2 cup vialone nano rice
1.5 litres milk
1 cup sugar
grated rind of 1 lemon
ground cinnamon

Put the rice and the cold milk in a heavy saucepan and bring to the boil, stirring all the time. Reduce the heat and simmer the rice for one hour, stirring from time to time to prevent it from sticking to the bottom of the saucepan. The rice should be well cooked and the mixture creamy. Add the sugar and lemon rind and, stirring all the time, cook the mixture until it comes to a simmer. Then cook the rice for a further five minutes. Pour the pudding into a large serving bowl, allow to cool, cover and refrigerate. Serve the rice in individual bowls sprinkled with ground cinnamon.

PULSES

Pulses include chickpeas, peas, beans and lentils — there is English pea soup, dhal from the subcontinent, refried beans from South America, soy bean tofu, hummus dips from North Africa and haricot beans in a French cassoulet.

The legume family is the third largest seed plant family in the world with around 18,000 species. Without legumes, life on Earth would not be as we know it today. A tiny bacteria that has a symbiotic relationship with legumes produces nitrogen in the soil in a much more efficient way than do fertilisers.

Pulses have a very long history. Lentils and broad beans have been discovered in settlements in Switzerland as early as the Bronze Age. In classical Greece and Rome pulses were eaten widely, and the Greeks and Romans knew both the benefits of crop rotation and that legume crops add fertility to the soil. In Homer's *Iliad*, Helenus's arrows bouncing off Menelaus's breastplate were compared to beans and chickpeas being thrown by the winnower. Ancient Egyptians used red lentils. Peas and beans were cultivated in Thailand from about 9750 BC and the Chinese have used soy beans throughout their cuisine. In the Americas pulses were an essential part of the diet from as early as 20,000 BC and the Aztecs were the first to grow some of the well-known beans of today.

ADZUKI BEANS are tiny, reddish-brown beans. Soak for 2–3 hours before boiling in fresh water for 15 minutes and simmering for about 45 minutes.

BLACK-EYED BEANS are native to tropical Africa and Asia and were taken to America with the slave trade. Soak for 2–3 hours before cooking in fresh water for about an hour.

BORLOTTI AND CANNELLINI BEANS are native to tropical

America and were introduced to Europe by the Spaniards. Soak overnight before cooking in fresh water for an hour or more.

BROAD BEANS, like lentils, are a very ancient food. Soak overnight before cooking in fresh water for an hour or more.

CHICKPEAS are used throughout the Mediterranean in soups and stews, for dips and as savouries. Soak overnight in three times their volume of water. Boil in fresh water for 10 minutes then simmer for an hour or more.

HARICOT AND FLAGEOLET BEANS are native to South America. They are often used in French and Italian dishes. Soak for 2–3 hours, boil in fresh water for 15 minutes then simmer for over an hour.

LENTILS can be large green and brown varieties or tiny red ones. Green lentils cook for 30–45 minutes. Red lentils cook in 10–15 minutes. Lentils are particularly good with pork, pork sausages and game, and make great soups and purées. But they are also being used in salads, especially the delicious, tiny lentilles du Puy, which are regarded as among the finest in the world and have a similar cooking time to red lentils.

PINTO AND RED KIDNEY BEANS were first cultivated by the Aztecs. Soak overnight. Boil in fresh water for 15 minutes then simmer covered for over one hour.

SOY BEANS are native to tropical Asia and have been the cornerstone of east Asian nutrition and cuisine for centuries. Soak overnight then boil in fresh water for 15 minutes and simmer covered for 2–3 hours.

YELLOW AND GREEN SPLIT PEAS were grown in Mesopotamia at least 5000 years ago. They are mostly used in soups and stews. Boil and skim the water, then simmer for 30–40 minutes.

STORAGE

Keep dried pulses in airtight containers in a cool, dry, dark place.

SALMON AND PUY LENTIL SALAD

Kate Lamont | Lamont's Wine & Food
serves 8–10

500g fresh salmon fillets
olive oil
500g lentilles du Puy
1 bulb garlic
1 bunch English spinach
1 cup flat leaf parsley
1 red onion
2 Ortiz anchovy fillets
50 ml vinegar
150 ml olive oil
1 cup semi-dried tomatoes, drained from the oil
salt and freshly ground pepper

Drizzle the salmon with olive oil and roast in the oven at 180°C until just cooked. Cool. Simmer the lentils for about 30 minutes in salted water until soft but not mushy. Drain and cool. Roast the whole garlic bulb until soft, about 20 minutes. Cool.

Wash and dry the spinach, roughly chop the parsley and finely slice the red onion.

Make a dressing by squeezing the roasted garlic from its skin and mashing it with the anchovy. Add the vinegar and drizzle in the olive oil while whisking.

Break the salmon fillet into large flakes. Mix all the ingredients together very gently. Season. Serve at room temperature with crusty bread and a light red wine.

BRUSCHETTA WITH CASTELLUCCIO DI NORCIA LENTILS

Antonio Carluccio

Place the lentils in a pot of cold water with chopped celery and cook for 30 minutes. Drain well and keep to one side. Grill both sides of slices of sourdough, then rub each side with a cut clove of garlic. Spread a tablespoon of the lentils on the bread with a sprig of rosemary a drizzle with extra virgin olive oil and season with sea salt.

Lentilles du Puy are grown on the volcanic soil of Le Puy in France and come with an Appellation d'Origine Contrôlée, the origin stamp of France which ensures their place of origin and their fine quality. The smaller lentils are, the better they taste; lentilles vertes du Puy are tiny, olive green in colour, marbled with steel blue. Their unique almond-flavoured skin is very soft so they don't need soaking. Lentilles du Puy retain their shape when cooked.
Even quicker-cooking lentils are those from Castelluccio di Norcia in Umbria, Italy, which are grown on the high plains at an altitude of 1500 metres. It's a very small production and only organic fertilisers are used on the plants. These are tiny, light green and brown striped legumes highly regarded by Italian cooks.

VINEGAR

GRAN DEPOSITO
TU BALSAMICO
DI
MODENA
SEPPE GIUSTI
NEL 160
ESPOSIZIONI

VINEGAR WAS USED BY THE EARLY EGYPTIANS, GREEKS AND ROMANS. ALTHOUGH USED MOSTLY AS A condiment, IT WAS ALSO VALUED FOR ITS medicinal PURPOSES. HIPPOCRATES PRESCRIBED IT FOR HIS PATIENTS, JULIUS CAESAR'S ARMIES drank VINEGAR MIXED WITH WATER AND AT ONE TIME IT WAS THOUGHT TO CURE SCURVY. IN THE middle AGES VINEGAR WAS THE CURSE OF MAKING wine, AS THE VINEGAR BACTERIA HAS BEEN KNOWN TO RUIN MANY A 'GREAT' WINE. HOWEVER, THERE HAVE BEEN (AND ARE) MANY GREAT WINE VINEGARS. IN 1394 THE guild OF PROFESSIONAL VINEGAR-MAKERS ESTABLISHED THE CORPORATIF DES MAITRES-VINAIGRIERS D'ORLEANS, IN ORLEANS, ONE OF THE major CENTRES OF THE FRENCH WINE TRADE.

Vinegar literally means sour wine (*vin aigre*), although the name is applied to vinegars made from beer, cider and grain alcohol as well. Any alcoholic liquid that contains less than 15 per cent alcohol (which most wine does) will become sour if exposed to the air. Early winemakers learned that wines had to be kept in full barrels at all times lest contact with the air change them into vinegar. They also discovered that a barrel of wine that had turned to vinegar 'soured' the barrel so that it could never be used for wine again.

HOW VINEGAR IS MADE

When the alcohol in wine comes into contact with the air, it oxidises into acetic acid. The oxidisation is greatly accelerated by a bacteria known as acetobacter which hastens a reaction between the alcohol and the newly formed acetic acid to form ethyl acetate. Ethyl acetate is what gives the fruity flavour in vinegar and acetic acid is what gives the tart taste; together they form the complex flavours of a good vinegar.

In the past the wine was allowed to undergo this process naturally. As the wine oxidises it causes a skin to form on the surface of the wine; this is called *Mycoderma aceti* or the 'vinegar mother'. A mother works in the same way as starter in sourdough bread; a little of it is added to fresh wine, along with some old vinegar and the souring process begins. More wine is added to the mother as it is depleted. Many famous vinegar makers use mothers that were started centuries ago. You may sometimes find a vinegar mother in a bottle of vinegar that you haven't used for some time — it will look like a jellyfish. You can use it to make your own vinegar from red or white wine. Today most vinegar makers add cultures that quickly dominate any wild organisms, bacteria or yeasts in the wine which could spoil the vinegar.

WINE VINEGAR

The best quality wine vinegars are made in barrels, using what is called the Orléans process. Chestnut or oak barrels are partially filled with good quality red or white wine — the better the wine, the better the

vinegar — and a quantity of old vinegar is added, along with a little of the vinegar mother. There are air holes in the sides of the barrels near the top which allow oxygen and acetobacter to convert the wine to vinegar. The process of making wine vinegar in this traditional way can take up to 12 months. The wine slowly turns acidic and develops flavour. The barrel maturation also adds complexity to the final vinegar — softening and enriching the flavour.

Commonly made wine vinegars: red wine, white wine, sherry and champagne.

STORAGE

All vinegars will deteriorate and should be sealed and kept in a cool, dark place.

STEAMED SURF CLAMS AND SAUCE VIERGE

Yvan Meunier | Boathouse
Serves 4

3 vine-ripened tomatoes
1 tablespoon coriander seeds
virgin olive oil
salt and freshly ground pepper
1/2 tablespoon parsley, chopped
1/2 tablespoon chives, chopped
1 1/2 tablespoons basil, chopped
1/2 tablespoon tarragon, chopped
2–3 tablespoons champagne vinegar
1 glass white wine
32 clams
mizuna leaves

Blanch and skin the tomatoes, remove the seeds and dice. Roast and grind the coriander seeds. Pass through a fine sieve and add to the diced tomatoes. Cover with virgin olive oil, season and add the chopped herbs. Add the champagne vinegar just before serving.

Heat a pot until very hot, then add the white wine and clams. Seal with a lid until all the clams are open. Serve the clams on some mizuna leaves with sauce poured over.

FLAVOURED VINEGARS

Flavoured vinegar is only as good as the vinegar that is used. Suitable herbs are thyme, rosemary, chives, fennel, tarragon, basil, mint, lemon balm and spices such as cloves, mustard seeds and peppercorns.

You can make your own flavoured vinegars by bringing vinegar to the boil and adding the herbs; simmer for about half an hour, then cool. Strain and bottle the vinegar. Put some herb sprigs in the bottle, use a skewer to arrange them before sealing the bottle. Store in a cool, dark cupboard.

SOLERO

Solero consists of a pyramid-shaped pile of barrels. The bottom barrels hold the newest vinegar, the top ones the oldest; slowly over the years the vinegar in the bottom barrels is moved up to the top ones. When new sherry is added to the lower barrels, some of the older vinegar is left in the barrel, so a good sherry vinegar, like balsamic vinegar, will always contain some old vinegar in its makeup.

WATER VINAIGRETTE

Matthew Fleming | CBD

Makes 700 ml

250 ml water
50 ml cabernet sauvignon vinegar
400 ml extra virgin olive oil
2 eschallots, finely sliced
3 sprigs of tarragon
sea salt and freshly ground white pepper
3 cloves garlic, peeled and thinly sliced

Combine the water and vinegar in a bowl. Add the olive oil, eschallots and tarragon. Season and lightly mix. Set aside for two hours to infuse the flavours. Strain through a fine sieve. Bring to a gentle boil in a saucepan with the garlic. Allow to cool, then strain. Use as a dressing for a salad of king prawns and chickpeas.

SHERRY VINEGAR

The best sherry vinegar comes from the home of the best sherry, Jerez in Spain. Jerez is one of the oldest Spanish wine producing towns. It may have been established by the Phoenicians as early as 1110BC. Its early name was Seris which evolved into Jerez.

There are three grape varieties grown in Jerez: Palomino, Pedro Ximénez and Muscat of Alexandria, with around 95 per cent of grapes being Palomino. Sherry vinegar is made from the fermented juice and is soured and aged using the same method as wine vinegar, except that a system called the solero is employed.

Solero is a system of fractional blending which maintains consistency of style. It takes its name from the barrels closest to the floor, or *suelo* from which the final blend is taken. The system smooths out the differences between vintage years and is a form of blending. Sherry vinegar is usually aged in barrels made from American oak. Sherry vinegar that is one year old is said to be good; 10 years old, excellent; 25 years old, outstanding; and 75 years old the equivalent of cognac.

RICOTTA AND ORANGE FRITTERS WITH GLAZED FIGS, DOUBLE CREAM, HONEY AND SHERRY VINEGAR SYRUP

Anthony Musarra | Lucciola

Serves 6

Fritters:

350g ricotta cheese

3 eggs, beaten

90g caster sugar

1 teaspoon orange zest

1 drop orange oil

pinch ground cinnamon

110g self-raising flour

Syrup:

100 ml sherry vinegar

200 ml water

100g caster sugar

1 cinnamon stick

50 ml honey

olive oil

9 ripe figs

caster sugar, extra

300 ml double cream

TO MAKE THE SYRUP: Place all the ingredients except the honey in a pot, then simmer over a medium heat until the syrup thickens and reduces slightly. Stir in the honey and leave to cool.

TO MAKE THE FRITTERS: Cream together the cheese, eggs, sugar, zest, orange oil and cinnamon. Blend in the flour. Cover until required. Heat some olive oil in a shallow pan over a medium heat. Spoon 1 tablespoon of the fritter mix into the oil. Cook four fritters at a time, on one side for about 3–4 minutes then carefully turn over and cook for another 3–4 minutes. When golden and cooked through lift from the oil and drain on paper towels.

Slice the figs in half lengthwise, dredge with caster sugar, then glaze under a hot grill or with a blow torch until the sugar caramelises.

Place two or three fritters on each plate with three fig halves. Put a large spoonful of cream on each plate, then pour some of the syrup on and around the dish.

OLD FASHIONED RABBIT FROM UMBRIA

Daryll Taylor | Jersey Cow
Serves 4

1 fresh rabbit, jointed
plain flour
6 tablespoons extra virgin olive oil
5 cloves garlic, chopped
1 bunch fresh sage, chopped
150 ml cider vinegar
150 ml hot water
freshly ground black pepper
60g salted capers, rinsed well and chopped
zest of 1 lemon, chopped
6 anchovy fillets, chopped

Wash and dry the rabbit pieces. Roll the rabbit pieces in flour and seal in a hot pan in the olive oil until golden brown. Remove from the pan.

Fry the garlic and sage for one minute. Add the rabbit pieces, the vinegar and hot water. Season with pepper, cover with a lid and cook gently for 40 minutes or until tender.

Remove the rabbit from the sauce and keep warm. Reduce the liquid by one-third and add the capers, lemon and anchovy fillets. Boil for one minute. Pour over the rabbit and serve with mashed or boiled potatoes.

BALSAMIC VINEGAR

Balsamic vinegar is made in Modena in the Emilia-Romagna region of Italy. It is not strictly a wine vinegar — it is made from the must (fresh juice) of white grapes, not wine. The one grape variety that is used to make the *vero balsamo* is the white Trebbiano grape, whose name is said to be derived from the grape's origins near the Trebbia river in Emilia-Romagna and from there was dispersed throughout Italy by the Roman Legionaries, becoming one of the most widely grown grape varieties in Italy.

The grapes are left on the vine for the longest possible time to achieve maximum sweetness. The must is cooked until it has reduced to a thick sweet syrup. It undergoes a fermentation process, then is poured into barrels with a little old vinegar and the vinegar mother. Each year as some of the vinegar evaporates, it is poured into smaller barrels, usually made from a different kind of wood. These barrels are highly valued — favourite woods are oak, mulberry, cherry, chestnut and juniper, each ancient wood imparting its own fragrance, colour and flavour to the developing vinegar. When the vinegar is transferred to a smaller barrel, a bit of the old vinegar from that barrel is left so the 'new' vinegar comes into contact with the old. As the balsamic evaporates it becomes more deeply flavoured, more richly coloured and more concentrated.

Balsamic vinegars may be aged for years, decades, even centuries; by the time it is ready to bottle, it is dark brown, slightly sweet and highly concentrated. Only after 12 years can it be labelled Aceto Balsamico Tradizionale di Modena and it must have been approved by a judging panel that ensures its quality. At 25 years or more it can be labelled Aceto Balsamico Tradizionale di Modena Extravecchio (very mature).

Balsamic vinegar's flavour is superb and the best way to taste it is to use it sparingly on simple food, such as a dish of sliced vine-ripened tomatoes. Mixed with extra virgin olive oil, balsamic vinegar makes a delicious vinaigrette for char-grilled vegetables and salads.

SIMON SAYS: THE OLDEST BALSAMIC VINEGAR IS LIKE TREACLE. IT IS CREDITED WITH RESTORATIVE POWERS, AND SOME OLD ITALIAN MEN LIKE TO TAKE A SMALL GLASS OF BALSAMIC AFTER DINNER, AS A DIGESTIF.

SHORTCUTS

Toss fresh strawberries in caster sugar and a few drops of balsamic.

A salad made from bitter greens topped with a poached egg is greatly improved with a little balsamic vinegar.

BRAISED PORTOBELLO MUSHROOMS WITH THYME, ROSEMARY AND BALSAMIC VINEGAR

Guillaume Brahimi | Quay
Serves 4

Pour a little olive oil into a baking dish and heat in preheated 180°C oven. Add 12 large Portobello mushrooms, sprinkle with some thyme and rosemary, and bake for about 20 minutes. When they are tender, slice them onto a plate. Deglaze the pan with a clove of finely chopped garlic, finely chopped parsley and balsamic vinegar and spoon the sauce over the mushrooms.

SIMON SAYS: LOOK FOR THE WORDS 'ACETO BALSAMICO DI MODENA' ON THE LABEL, WHICH GUARANTEES THE VINEGAR WAS MADE IN THE MODENA REGION.

VERJUICE

Verjuice is made from the juice of unripe grapes, which is what gives it a high acidity. Its use dates back to the Middle Ages and it is a common ingredient in the grape producing areas of Europe.

The grapes are picked while still very green. The high acid and low sugar content gives the verjuice its characteristic sharp acidic flavour. If the grapes are sweet and juicy enough to eat then they are too ripe.

The grapes are crushed and the juice is extracted using the same process as for white wine, but instead of fermenting the juice it is cold stabilised and filtered. These processes stop the growth of wild yeasts or bacteria in the juice which would make it volatile.

Verjuice adds a fresh sharp flavour with a hint of grape to dishes and can be used wherever a light vinegar would be used. Use it in salad dressings, sauces or to deglaze a pan.

MAGGIE BEER'S VERJUICE
(Barossa Valley, South Australia)

Maggie Beer first experimented with making verjuice in 1973 when some of their vineyard's grapes were not required. The first batches were made from riesling grapes but as time has gone on sylvaner and gordo grapes have also been used.

The classic use for verjuice is to add it to soup, stock or sauces to give extra depth to the flavours.

VERJUICE VINAIGRETTE FOR BITTER GREENS

Maggie Beer

Makes 3/4 cup

2 tablespoons verjuice
2 teaspoons lemon juice
1/2 cup walnut oil
sea salt and freshly ground black pepper

Mix together and serve with a salad of bitter greens, freshly shelled walnuts, garlic and grapes.

SHORTCUTS

Maggie Beer

Brush wild or cultivated mushrooms with walnut oil and verjuice and barbecue.

Plunge freshly barbecued quail or chicken pieces in a bath of verjuice, fresh herbs and olive oil while they rest.

Soak pears, quinces or dried fruit in verjuice before poaching.

CONDIMENTS

SALT, pepper, CAPERBERRIES, CHILLIES, CITRUS RIND, honey,

MUSTARD, PIMIENTO, PRESERVED LEMON, SAFFRON, SALICORNES, SUGAR, VANILLA

— CONDIMENTS PLAY A CRUCIAL ROLE IN EVERY cuisine. WHO COULD

imagine A MEXICAN TORTILLA WITHOUT CHILLIES, A MERINGUE WITHOUT

SUGAR OR AN ANCHOVY WITHOUT SALT? THEY WOULD HARDLY RESEMBLE THEIR

FORMER SELVES! CONDIMENTS ARE AT THE VERY HEART OF THE KITCHEN, PLAYING

MANY INTRIGUING ROLES — THEY FORM BITING contrasts AND LONG-

STANDING RELATIONSHIPS; THEY PRESERVE THINGS, ENHANCE FLAVOURS; THEY

EVEN PLAY A PART IN MEDICINAL COMPOUNDS. THERE ARE MANY classic

PARTNERSHIPS: THE bite OF CAPERBERRIES WITH TUNA IN A SALAD NICOISE;

PUNGENT, AROMATIC SAFFRON WITH RICE IN PAELLA (WHICH ALSO FLAGS ANOTHER

GREAT COMBINATION: SAFFRON AND SEAFOOD); AND PERFUMED vanilla WITH

CREAM IN CREME BRULEE. SOMETIMES SIMPLE, OTHER TIMES MORE COMPLEX,

EVERY cuisine HAS ITS STOREHOUSE OF INVENTIVE USES FOR CONDIMENTS.

SALT

The salt production methods employed by the Romans in Britain were ingeniously simple. They collected saturated brine from natural springs, then they evaporated this brine in open pans over a fire to retrieve the salt crystals. Salt mines have been in existence since the Bronze Age and evaporation of sea water in shallow lakes and salt pans to collect salt goes back centuries too. Venice extracted salt from its lagoons and a great deal of the city's prosperity and future dominance of the spice trade grew from this beginning. Brine evaporation is still the basic principle of salt production today.

Salting was probably the major method used to preserve food before refrigeration — it was used to slow down or prevent bacterial growth.

Most of the salt we buy today is refined, that is, coated with chemicals to keep the grains separate and free running. These chemicals give salt, particularly iodised salt, a somewhat bitter taste. Unrefined sea salt, on the other hand, is completely natural, produced by evaporation of sea water, with no chemicals or additives, and as a result it has a sweeter taste. You'll find you use less of it than refined salt. Sea salt is used throughout the world every day to preserve food, to enhance flavours and flavour food.

The soft crystals should be served in a little salt cellar on the table; crush them between your fingers. Try it on a simple tomato salad, or a steaming baked potato with a slice of cold unsalted butter and you'll taste the difference at once. Sprinkled over bread or pretzels before you put them in the oven, the salt retains its crunchiness. Remember to return it to an airtight container because unrefined salt absorbs moisture from the air.

SIMON SAYS: I REMEMBER TRYING FLEUR DE SEL FOR THE FIRST TIME AND THINKING IT WAS THE BEST SALT I HAD EVER HAD.

SALINES DE GUERANDE

Brittany, France

Salines de Guérande is found in the marshes near the medieval town of Guérande in Brittany, France. Salt crystals gather in thick white sheets on the marshes, giving the area the name 'white country'. It is raked off in a time-honoured way by *paludière*, female salt-pan workers, who are considered the only people nimble enough to perform this delicate task.

FLEUR DE SEL

The finest first layer of salt crystals, known as Fleur de Sel (flower salt, because its subtle aroma has a hint of violets), is neither washed nor ground; it is simply dried, and in this way preserves its natural brinish taste.

GRIS TRADITION

A coarser salt collected from the bottom of the marshes is Gris Tradition; off-white in colour with big grains, it too has no artificial additions. It is perfect for cooking and it can also be used at the table with a special salt grinder.

SHORTCUT

Preserved lemons

These are whole lemons which have been pickled in sea salt. They have lost most of their bitterness but none of their lemony flavour. Rinse before using to get rid of excess salt, cut away and discard the pulp — only the peel is used.

Cut a vertical cross almost through to the base of the lemon. Insert coarse salt into the cuts. Press each lemon closed and place in a sterilised jar. Pack them tightly. Top up the jar with lemon juice. Seal and place in a cool dark cupboard for at least four weeks. To use, rinse well, discard the flesh and use the peel as required.

PAILLARD OF CHICKEN BREAST WITH PRESERVED LEMONS, COUSCOUS AND PISTACHIO BUTTER

Andrew Blake | Blakes
Serves 6

50g pistachio nuts
1 birdseye chilli
160g unsalted butter
3 tablespoons parsley, chopped
3 tablespoons pomegranate seeds
2 shallots, minced
Boyajian garlic oil
olive oil
375 ml chicken stock
300g instant couscous
3 tablespoons preserved lemons, diced
salt and freshly ground pepper
3 double chicken breasts

TO MAKE THE PISTACHIO BUTTER: Roast the pistachio nuts and chilli until lightly browned. Place in a food processor and pulse; then place in a bowl and mix with the unsalted butter and parsley.

TO MAKE THE POMEGRANATE SYRUP: Pureé the pomegranate seeds and strain. Reduce the liquid over a low heat until it forms a syrup.

TO MAKE THE COUSCOUS: Sauté the shallots in the garlic oil for five minutes. Add the chicken stock and remove from the heat. Pour this mixture over the couscous and stir. Put it aside for 10 minutes or until the couscous has absorbed the liquid. Add the preserved lemon peel.

Char-grill the chicken. Reheat the couscous and divide it between six plates. Place the chicken on the couscous and top with a spoonful of pistachio butter. Drizzle with the pomegranate syrup.

PEPPER

If you could take only one spice to a desert island, it would probably be pepper — nothing compares to the aromatic hit of freshly ground pepper. On the consumer price index it is one food that has come down in value; during the Crusades, a kilo of peppercorns was worth about six weeks labour on the land. In the fifteenth century pepper-corns became a valuable currency, hence the term 'peppercorn rent', which meant the opposite of what it means today.

All pepper comes from *Piper nigrum*, a perennial vine with shiny, dark green leaves that grows to 10 metres or more in height. It orig-inated in tropical west India and is now grown throughout the tropics. The unripe fruit is green, turning greenish yellow, then red, as it ripens.

BLACK PEPPERCORNS: Green unripe berries are harvested and left in heaps to ferment for a few days, then spread on mats to dry in the sun until they shrivel and turn black.

WHITE PEPPERCORNS: Greenish yellow peppercorns are soaked in water then macerated to rub off the outer hull and dried in the sun until creamy white. They have more bite and less aroma than black pepper, which is useful when you don't want black specks in a sauce.

PINK PEPPERCORNS: Fully ripe red peppercorns are preserved in brine. Good in terrines, or with game.

SZECHUAN PEPPERCORNS (CHINESE PEPPER): These are not true pepper, but a pod from the prickly ash. They are a good companion to sea salt and black pepper.

SZECHUAN PEPPER AND SALT

Kylie Kwong

Combine three parts sea salt and one part Szechuan peppercorns in a mixing bowl. Dry roast until the mixture begins to brown. Remove and grind the spices to a powder.

MUSSEL, RIESLING & CURRY BROTH

Jeremy Strode | Pomme
Serves 4

vegetable oil
2 brown onions, peeled and chopped
4 cloves garlic, finely sliced
1 celery stick, chopped
4 sprigs thyme
6 parsley stalks
1 teaspoon white peppercorns
60 mussels, washed and beards removed
250 ml riesling
150 ml very cold unsalted butter, chopped
2 teaspoons curry powder
200 ml pure cream
1 tomato, blanched, peeled and diced
50g white radish, peeled, diced and blanched
1/4 bunch chives, chopped finely
1 Fuji apple, peeled, cored and chopped
freshly ground white pepper

Heat some oil in a deep, thick-bottomed pan. Add half the chopped onions with the garlic, celery, thyme, parsley and peppercorns and stir through. Add the mussels and the riesling and cover tightly. Cook over a high heat until the mussels just open. Strain, reserving the mussel liquor, and cover the mussels with a damp cloth.

In another pan, melt a knob of the butter, add the remaining onion and cook until soft but not coloured. Add the curry powder and cook, stirring, over a low heat for 10 minutes.

Add the mussel liquor and bring to the boil. Add the cream, re-boil and simmer for five minutes. Meanwhile, remove the mussels from the shells and cover.

To serve, divide the mussels between four warm soup plates. Sprinkle with the tomato, radish, chives, apple and pepper. Using a processor, blend the curry broth with the remaining butter to achieve a froth. Pour gently over the mussels and serve immediately.

SPICED QUINCES COOKED IN A SUGAR SYRUP

Colin Holt

Serves 8

8 quinces

Sugar syrup:
1.5 kg white sugar
2 litres water
3 cinnamon quills
2 teaspoons cracked black peppercorns
10 cloves
6 fresh bay leaves
1 lemon, cut in half

To make the sugar syrup: Place all the ingredients into a stainless steel pot and bring to the boil. Remove from the heat.

Cut the quinces into quarters and peel off the skin. Using a small knife, carefully remove the cores. Place the cores in a square of muslin and tie with string.

Place the quinces and cores in the sugar syrup. Bring to the boil and cover with greaseproof paper, and weigh down the quinces with a smaller lid to keep them under the liquid. Place the pot in a 100°C oven for approximately 6–8 hours, or longer if needed, until the quinces are a dark purple.

Allow the quinces to cool in the syrup. Place the quinces with the syrup into sealed jars, as they can be stored for a long time. Use for tarts and as a garnish for other dishes.

CHILLI

The chilli pepper has become, after salt and sugar, the most frequently used condiment in the world. Chillies are native to the Americas and were introduced to Europe around 1500 by the Spanish, and to Asia and India by the Portuguese, following their visits to South America. Chillies had been cultivated in Mexico as early as 5000 BC. Virtually all the chillies that are found in markets around the world are *Capsicum annuum*. There are untold numbers of varieties of this species. Just some of the better known ones are:

BANANA CHILLIES: Pale-yellow to yellow large, sweet and hot chillies.

BIRD'S EYE: Red, glossy, tiny, very hot chillies.

JALAPEÑO: Red, cylindrical, hot to very hot chillies — the best known chilli in North America.

PEPPERONCINI: Green, elongated and wrinkled chillies used in Italian pickles. The name comes from the Italian word for chilli, *peperone*.

PIMENTO: Green to red, glossy, conical shape — the name comes from the Spanish word *pimiento*. It has an aromatic flavour.

THAI CHILLIES: Dark green to red, long, narrow, hot chillies.

PRIK BON (ROASTED CHILLI POWDER)

David Thompson | Darley Street Thai

1 cup dried bird'seye chillies (or large dried red chillies)

Roast the chillies in a wok or pan over a medium heat until they have changed colour and are beginning to toast. Stir regularly to prevent them scorching. Be careful not to inhale the fumes. Cool, then grind to coarse or fine powder. Prik bon will keep well in an airtight container.

PAPRIKA

Paprika or pimientón is a finely ground powder made from dried sweet peppers of the chilli family. The mild sweet variety is the one most often encountered, but there is also a bittersweet type and a spicy paprika. Use Spanish pimientón in Spanish and Mediterranean seafood dishes, and the Hungarian paprika in dishes such as goulash and in potato and vegetable soups and stews. Store in an airtight container.

SAFFRON POTATOES

Anthony Musarra | Lucciola

Serves 6

1 small onion, peeled and chopped finely

1 clove garlic, peeled and crushed

extra virgin olive oil

1 teaspoon La Chinata bitter/sweet pimientón

18 small kipfler or desirée potatoes

200 ml chicken stock

2–3g saffron threads

salt

freshly ground black pepper

Cook the onion and garlic in a pan with a little olive oil until soft. Add the piementón then cook another 2–3 minutes. Add the potatoes and toss over medium heat till the potatoes are evenly coated. Add the stock, saffron, a little salt and pepper then cover and simmer approximately 20 minutes so the potatoes are tender. Serve with lamb cutlets and a Romesco sauce.

LA CHINATA
(Spain)

The La Chinata company in the La Vera region of Spain prides itself on the traditional drying process it uses to produce its pimiento. The peppers are dried very slowly for 10 to 15 days over a hearth of oak. They are turned over and over and the heat and smoke dehydrate the peppers and impart flavour. The peppers' stalks and some of the seeds are removed (the number of seeds retained determines the spiciness of the paprika), and they are ground to a fine powder in traditional stone mills.

SIMON SAYS: LA CHINATA HAS THE RESPECTED DO (DENOMINACIÓN DE ORIGEN) STAMP, WHICH GUARANTEES ITS AUTHENTICITY.

PIQUILLO PIMIENTOS

Piquillo peppers are grown in Navarra, Spain in limited numbers. They are roasted over beech wood, hand-peeled and packed with only their own juices — no water is added. Those produced by Conservas el Nararrico have the DO stamp (Denominación de Origen), the official Spanish government stamp which ensures the highest quality. Enteros are whole pimientos; En Tiras are cut into pieces.

Lew Kathreptis
Serves 4

extra virgin olive oil
6 cloves garlic, peeled and chopped
8 red chillies, seeded and julienned
150g pimientos, chopped
1 bunch basil, torn
juice of 2 lemons
1/4 cup tiny capers
3/4 cup grated parmigiano reggiano
1 ricotta, crumbled
1 kg spaghetti, cooked

Heat the oil in a pan and sauté the garlic. Add the chilli and cook briefly. In a bowl combine pimientos, basil, lemon juice, capers, half a cup of the parmigiano reggiano and the ricotta. Add the garlic mixture in the pan, then stir through the cooked spaghetti. Serve with the remaining grated parmesan.

MUSTARD

The different seeds of the mustard plant provide the basis for mustard: white, *Sinapis alba*; brown, *Brassica juncea*; and black, *Brassica nigra*. The blend of these seeds with herbs and spices forms the basis of most prepared mustards. The intense flavour of mustard is due to an essential oil found in the seeds. Mustard is at its best if eaten uncooked. In sauces and other hot foods, it loses its heat and flavour if cooked for too long. For best results, add it only at the final stages of cooking.

DIJON MUSTARD

Dijon mustard is the world's most famous mustard and the one to choose if you have only one mustard in your cupboard. Mix it into mayonnaise and vinaigrette, or use it in creamy mustard sauce. Dijon mustard is a mixture of black mustard seeds (*Brassica nigra*) without their seed husk, salt, spices and white wine or verjuice.

TRUFFLE OIL VINAIGRETTE

Russell Armstrong | Armstrong's Brisbane
Makes 3 cups

6 shallots, finely sliced
1 pickled onion, finely sliced
20g Dijon mustard
60 ml sherry vinegar
180 ml truffle oil
80 ml truffle juice
180 ml olive oil
20 ml sherry
15 ml brandy
20 ml Madeira
100g bacon lardons, small and cooked (omit for vegetarians)
salt and freshly ground pepper

Combine all the ingredients and adjust the seasoning.

CAPERS

Capers are the small unopened flower buds of a spiny shrub that grows wild in Mediterranean regions. Capers are expensive because the buds have to be picked by hand at just the right time in their development; the smaller they are, the sweeter and more tender. They are preserved in salt or salted vinegar. Caperberries are the pollinated fruit of the caper bush, sold with their stalk attached and preserved in brine.

Capers may be cooked or eaten just as they are. Salted capers should be rinsed well before using. Fry them in oil, drain, then toss over a salad or add them to mayonnaise-based sauces or in sauces to serve with fish. They are particularly good with tuna, especially in niçoise

salad, and vitello tonnato, the Italian dish of cold cooked veal with tuna sauce.

TUNA, POTATO AND SARDINE SALAD WITH CAPERBERRIES

Sherry Clewlow

Slice 4 medium desirée potatoes into thin discs. Coat generously with extra virgin olive oil and season with salt and pepper. Bake at 180°C until golden brown. Dust 16 fresh sardine fillets with flour and lightly fry in a little olive oil. Drain 200g tuna from its oil and break into flakes. Drain 100g caperberries and marinate in extra virgin olive oil with a dash of balsamic vinegar. Layer the potatoes, sardines and tuna with rocket and top with drained caperberries. Sprinkle with either a Caesar dressing or a thin salsa verde.

SHORTCUT

Toss together black olives, rinsed capers, grilled cherry tomatoes and finely sliced green onions. Mix with extra virgin olive oil and a dash of balsamic vinegar and serve as a chunky salsa with seared tuna steaks.

SALICORNES

Salicornes are the chopped tender shoots of a marine plant that grows in the salty marshes of Brittany. The plant is picked by hand when still young. The jointed shoot is broken up and either bottled in salt water (*au naturel*) or pickled in a marinade of white wine vinegar, onions, carrots and pepper (*à la marinade*). Salicornes have a crunchy texture. Natural salicornes should be drained and rinsed before using.

SHORTCUT

Fry salicornes with butter, garlic and parsley and serve with veal, fish, pork or scrambled eggs. Drain salicornes à la marinade and serve with cold meats, fish and salads.

SAFFRON

This is the world's most expensive spice, and no wonder: it takes about 250,000 *Crocus sativus* flowers to harvest one kilogram of saffron. And it is all done by hand. Each flower is individually picked and its three hair-like stigmas are individually removed from the flower and dried — and that's what saffron is. These orange–red threads, about 4 cm long, impart a strong yellow colour to food and a unique honey-like taste.

Traditionally saffron is used in rice dishes, particularly paella, pilau and risotto, but it is also an important ingredient in bouillabaisse and many other Mediterranean dishes. English cooks use saffron in cakes, and it is used in Kashmiri and other northern Indian dishes. It keeps well if stored in an airtight container.

To use saffron, infuse a few threads in a little hot water for 2–4 hours and add the liquid towards the end of cooking; or toast the strands lightly in a dry pan and, when crisp, crush them with the back of a spoon; or fry them in oil or butter before adding to the dish. The best saffron is said to come from Spain, but it is also produced in Iran, Turkey, Kashmir, and recently, Tasmania.

SIMON SAYS: A SIMPLE WAY TO TEST FOR REAL SAFFRON IS TO MIX IT WITH A LITTLE ALCOHOL. IF THE ALCOHOL TURNS YELLOW, IT IS NOT SAFFRON.

FILLET OF SNAPPER WITH ARTICHOKE, SAFFRON, TOMATO AND CAPERS

Liam Tomlin | Banc
Serves 4

120 ml extra virgin olive oil
20 pieces marinated artichoke heart
pinch of saffron threads
4 x 160g fillets of baby snapper, scaled and boned
salt and freshly ground pepper
lemon juice
4 heads baby bok choy with leaves separate and washed
30g salted capers, well rinsed
2 large vine ripened tomatoes, blanched, peeled, de-seeded and diced large
chervil sprigs

In a saucepan gently warm the oil, add the artichokes and saffron and allow to warm through slowly.

Season the fish with salt and pepper and cook in a little oil in a large cast iron pan, skin side down, until the skin is crisp and golden brown. Turn the fish and cook flesh side down for 30 seconds. Season with a squeeze of lemon juice.

While the fish is cooking, cook the bok choy in boiling salted water and drain, season lightly. Add the capers and tomato to the oil, add lemon juice and ground pepper to taste.

Place the bok choy in the centre of each of the four plates, drizzle over a little olive oil. Spoon the artichokes around the bok choy. Place a fillet of snapper in the centre of each plate and scatter with chervil leaves.

SUGAR

Sugar can be traced back several thousand years in China and India. Soldiers of the Persian Emperor Darius saw sugar cane growing on the banks of the River Indus. They called it 'the reeds which produce honey without bees'.

Much later it was grown in Persia and the Arabs took it to Egypt. The word sugar is itself derived from an Arabic word. By 600 AD the practice of breaking up the sugar cane and boiling it to produce sugar crystals was widespread. Six hundred years later, when Marco Polo visited China, he saw flourishing sugar mills.

From the Middle Ages on, sugar was for several centuries a commodity a little like pepper in price and usage. King Henry III of England had difficulty in obtaining as much as one and a half kilograms for a banquet in 1226.

By the middle of the fifteenth century there were plantations in Madeira, the Canary Islands and St Thomas, and they supplied Europe with sugar until the sixteenth century, when manufacture spread to America, followed by the West Indies.

GRANULATED: This is the standard refined white sugar with medium sized crystals.

CASTER: Caster sugar is produced by screening fine white crystals from granulated sugar. Because it is finer and dissolves faster than ordinary white sugar, it is particularly useful for cake mixtures and puddings.

CUBE: Damp white sugar is pressed into moulds and the moulds dried, making the crystals stick together.

BROWN SUGARS:

The brown colour comes from sugar cane molasses which also imparts a very special flavour. Brown sugars range in colour from

Light Golden Brown (low molasses content) through Siúcra Demerara (medium molasses content) to Rich Dark Brown (high molasses content). Brown sugars are very useful in many cakes and puddings.

ANTILLAISE: a fine-grained brown sugar which is the best sugar for crème brûlée. It melts to a beautiful caramel topping.

RAW SUGAR (OR GOLDEN GRANULATED): This is a free-flowing brown sugar containing cane molasses, which gives it a unique flavour.

QUARTZ AMBRE: This is a golden sugar, made using a slow crystallisation process which causes diamond-shaped crystals to form, perfect for coffee.

GOLDEN SYRUP AND TREACLE: These are syrups with the characteristic colour, flavour and aroma of sugar cane molasses.

Sugar is used as a sweetener, as a preservative in jams, preserves and for fruits, for enhancing flavour in foods such as preserved meats and tomato sauce and for confectionery.

CHOCOLATE DESSERT

Michael Lambie | CIRCA' the prince

Serves 4

Base:
250 ml milk
25g cornflour
25g cocoa powder
50g sugar
4 egg yolks
40g Valrohna chocolate, melted

Soufflé:
400 ml egg whites
20g sugar
400g soufflé base

TO MAKE THE SOUFFLE BASE: Bring the milk to the boil. Remove from the heat. Mix together the cornflour, cocoa powder, sugar and egg yolks. Stir the mixture into the boiled milk. Gently heat, stirring all the time until the mixture coats the back of a spoon. Pour into a bowl and whisk. Add the melted chocolate and continue to whisk until the mixture begins to cool.

TO MAKE THE SOUFFLE: Whisk the egg whites and the sugar until soft peaks form. Gently warm the soufflé base in a separate bowl over a saucepan of boiling water. Fold in one-third of the meringue and mix lightly until smooth. Fold in the rest of the meringue.

Grease four ceramic ramekins with butter and then coat with sugar. Fill the ramekins to two-thirds full. Smooth off the top and bake in a preheated convection oven at 210°C for approximately 10-12 minutes.

Dust lightly with icing sugar and serve hot with a scoop of ice cream.

SUGAR SYRUP FOR POACHING
Heat 2 parts water and 1 part sugar, stirring occasionally until the sugar has dissolved.

SUGAR SYRUP FOR SORBETS
Heat equal quantities of sugar and water, stirring occasionally to dissolve the sugar. Boil for five minutes and allow to cool.

CARAMEL
Boil 1 part water to 4 parts sugar and stir until the sugar has dissolved. Stop stirring once the syrup is clear. Continue to cook until a rich caramel colour. Remove from the heat and cool.

CANDIED ORANGE AND CEDRO (CITRON) PEEL

Candied peel is made in the same way as glacé fruits: cooked in a sugar syrup of increasing strength. The best candied peel is cooked in big pieces and then cut into strips. In this way no essential oils are lost and the peel remains soft and juicy. Cedro is the Italian name for citron, a large greenish-yellow citrus fruit that looks like a lumpy lemon. It has very thick peel and is mostly used for candying—cooked very slowly over a long period of time. Store the candied peel in air-tight jars.

SHORTCUTS

Dip candied peel in melted chocolate and serve with coffee.

Slice candied cedro thinly and serve it with cheese.

Chop candied oranges and whisk into mascarpone.

ORANGE POT-AU-CRÈME

Greg Doyle | Pier
Serves 12

750 ml heavy cream (45%)
250g sugar
8 egg yolks
50 ml Cointreau

Orange sauce:
6 blood oranges
250g caster sugar
250 ml still mineral water

5–6 blood oranges, peeled and segmented
orange sorbet

Heat the cream and sugar in a saucepan, stirring until the sugar dissolves and the cream is quite warm. Make sure the cream does not get too hot or boil. Put the egg yolks in a bowl and whisk together, making sure the mixture does not foam. Pour the hot cream into the egg yolk mixture, a little at a time, stirring constantly. Strain through a fine sieve and add the Cointreau. Pour the mixture into little pots, making sure to fill the pots right to the top. Place the pots in a baking dish and pour in hot water to halfway up the sides of the pots. Cover with foil and bake in a preheated 175°C oven for about 30 minutes or until set. The custard should still be a little wobbly in the centre. Remove from the oven and cool on a rack.

To make the sauce: Carefully peel the zest from the oranges with a vegetable peeler. Make sure that there is no pith on the zest. Slice the zest into julienne strips. Halve the oranges and juice them. Strain the juice and place in a saucepan with the sugar and water. Heat and stir until the sugar has dissolved. Add the orange zest and bring to the boil. Boil until the sauce has reduced and thickened to a heavy syrup. Chill.

Serve each pot-au-crème with 5 or 6 blood orange segments drizzled with sauce and a scoop of orange sorbet.

PURE LIGURIAN BEE HONEY
Kangaroo Island, off the coast of South Australia, is thought to contain the last strain of pure Ligurian bees in the world. Established in the 1880s as a bee sanctuary, there's been no cross-breeding of the bees, so they produce pure Ligurian honey, renowned for its fine quality and rich butterscotch taste.

HONEY

Honey is the world's oldest sweetener. The ancient Greeks and Romans used it to sweeten bread, and this led to the creation of a whole range of honey-spice cakes, including English gingerbread. The aristocrats of honey are single flower honeys.

NOUGAT

Nougat or torrone is made with roasted peeled almonds or hazelnuts, honey and candied fruit. It is enclosed in paper-thin edible rice paper. It can be soft and chewy (*morbido*), or brittle (*friabile*). Torrone was known in ancient Roman times, and nowadays in made in many regions: Piedmont, Lombardy, Sicily, Campania, Abruzzi (which makes a special chocolate-flavoured variety) and Tuscany.

HONEY ANGLAISE

Heat 300 ml of milk, 300 ml of cream, 100g of sugar and 1 tablespoon of honey in a heavy pan. Stir until sugar has dissolved. Beat six egg yolks in a large bowl and pour the hot (not boiling) mixture over them, whisking constantly. Return the mixture to the pan and stir over a very low heat until it coats the back of a spoon. If the custard gets too hot, it will curdle. Remove from the heat. Serve with fresh fruit or freshly made hot gingerbread.

VANILLA

The vanilla plant is a climbing orchid that takes two and a half years to start bearing fruit. The pods are harvested while still unripe; at this stage they have no vanilla taste. They are dipped in boiling water and then packed in boxes to sweat at night, and are exposed to the sun by day. This process takes about ten days. Then the bean pods are spread on trays in an airy shelter until they are dry enough for grading and packing, the whole curing and drying process takes about five months. At the end of this time they are black, glossy and still supple and moist.

The best vanilla beans are covered with a white frosting of vanillin crystals which forms as the vanilla beans cure and which is highly aromatic. The word 'vanillin' has become confusing because synthetic vanillin can be made and is often used as an artificial flavouring in chocolate. Real vanilla extract is made by crushing the cured dried vanilla beans and steeping them in alcohol — an expensive process that is reflected in the price. In the best vanilla essence no sugar is added.

Store vanilla beans in a jar of caster sugar. Use the sugar to flavour cakes, ice creams and puddings and keep topping up the sugar as you use it. The vanilla beans will continue flavouring the sugar for about a year. Or, cut the beans lengthways, scrape out the seeds and put the beans and seeds into milk or cream as you heat it to make ice cream or puddings. This will produce a strongly flavoured cream with the characteristic little black flecks that show real vanilla has been used.

VANILLA PARFAIT

Daryll Taylor | Jersey Cow
Serves 4

175g caster sugar
125 ml water
7 egg yolks
1 whole egg
1 vanilla pod, split and scraped
550 ml cream

Combine the sugar and water in a small saucepan and slowly bring
to the boil. Continue boiling for approximately five minutes until
the soft ball stage. Meanwhile place the egg yolks, whole egg and the
vanilla pod scrapings in a mixer and whisk for 30 seconds. Slowly
pour in the sugar syrup and whisk until cold. Whip the cream and
fold into the mixture. Pour the mixture into a mould and freeze for
eight hours. Unmould and slice to serve.

CHOCOLATE

WHAT IS IT THAT MAKES SOME chocolate SO EXQUISITE? IT ALL STARTS

WITH THE COCOA (CACAO) TREE, WHICH PRODUCES COCOA BEANS. THE cocoa

TREE CAN ONLY BE GROWN IN EQUATORIAL REGIONS, BETWEEN THE TROPIC OF

CANCER AND THE tropic OF CAPRICORN. THE POD IS THE FRUIT OF THESE

TREES. ABOUT 30 OR 40 BEANS THE SIZE OF AN almond ARE FOUND IN

EACH POD; THE CHARACTERISTICS OF THE beans VARY ACCORDING TO THEIR

PARTICULAR variety AND WHERE THEY'RE GROWN — A VARIETY GROWN IN

SOUTH AMERICA WILL TASTE VERY DIFFERENT TO THE SAME VARIETY grown IN

THE CARIBBEAN.

There are three major categories of cocoa bean: *forastero*, *criollo* and *trinitario*. *Criollo* and *trinitario* are the best and the rarest (85 per cent of chocolate is made from *forastero* beans) so, to make a really good chocolate, you must use *criollo* and *trinitario* beans.

After the pods are harvested, the beans and the white mucilage that surrounds them are scraped out and fermented. Small growers do this by making piles of the beans and mucilage and covering them with banana leaves; larger estates use wooden 'sweat-boxes'. Fermentation gets rid of the beans' bitterness. The beans are dried, preferably in the sun, which takes about a week. Beans that have been artificially dried in drying rooms with heat generated by gasoline or coal have an unpleasant smoky taste. And it's pervasive — a tiny number of artificially dried cocoa beans can spoil a bagful.

Once dried the beans are shipped to the chocolate manufacturer, where they are roasted and blended. The outer skins of the beans are removed, leaving what is known as the nibs. These are ground to a paste and some of the cocoa butter is removed under pressure, leaving a paste called chocolate liquor. Sugar is added to the liquor with cocoa butter and flavourings such as vanilla, lecithin (for a smooth texture) and milk powder or condensed milk for milk chocolate.

Now the mixture is ready for conching, the process where the chocolate mixture is poured into a big drum that rotates like a concrete mixer, blending and smoothing the mixture and at the same time mellowing the flavour. This can take from 12 to 100 hours depending on the quality. The longer the conching, the smoother and more flavoursome the chocolate. After conching the chocolate is tempered (heated and then cooled) to give it a glossy appearance, then it is poured into moulds.

TYPES OF CHOCOLATE

BITTERSWEET/PLAIN/DARK: Good-quality bittersweet chocolate will contain a high percentage of cocoa — from about 35–71 per cent — and be lightly sweetened.

MILK: This contains milk powder or condensed milk and usually has a lower percentage of cocoa than bittersweet chocolate, but more sugar.

WHITE: Made from cocoa butter and milk, it contains no chocolate liquor, which is why it is white.

COUVERTURE: This describes commercial quantities of chocolate, generally used for cooking. It is usually but not always made from high quality chocolate, and is widely available as both bittersweet and milk.

COMPOUND: Avoid this at all costs. Much of the cocoa butter has been replaced with other fats such as coconut oil, which totally spoils its taste and texture.

COOKING WITH CHOCOLATE

The best chocolate to cook with is the finest eating chocolate. Melt chocolate slowly in a double boiler or bowl over a pan of simmering water. It can also be melted in the microwave at 50 per cent power, but remember that it retains its shape when heated in the microwave and you only know it's melted when you stir it. Watch that no water gets into the chocolate or it will 'seize', i.e. form a clump and harden. Unless you have a supply of cocoa butter with which to bring it back, you'll have to throw it out and start again.

SIMON SAYS: MANY PEOPLE ASSUME THAT IF A CHOCOLATE HAS A HIGH PERCENTAGE OF COCOA IT MUST BE GOOD, BUT IT WILL ONLY BE GOOD IF THE COCOA BEANS ARE GOOD IN THE FIRST PLACE AND IF THE PERCENTAGE OF COCOA IS APPROPRIATE TO THAT BEAN.

CHOCOLATE SAUCE

Lorraine Godsmark

Cut 200g Valrhona chocolate (Manjari) into small pieces. Bring 125 ml water and 125 ml cream to the boil. Pour over the chocolate and stir well. The sauce can be stored in the refrigerator and reheated over a bain marie when required.

VALRHONA

Valrhona chocolates are labelled according to their cocoa content and the beans' country of origin as well as their bean variety or blend. Valrhona buy the best cocoa beans (*criollo* and *trinitario*), and they only buy beans that are dried in the sun. They roast the beans from each region separately to allow for variations in temperature and time, and according to variety, and only then do they blend the beans. (Most chocolate manufacturers blend the beans first and roast them all together.)

Valrhona grind their chocolate exceedingly fine, which helps to give the chocolate its smooth velvety texture.

Conching is done for more than 100 hours — some chocolate manufacturers conch for only 12 hours. Conching develops the flavour and makes the chocolate smooth and creamy.

VALRHONA

GRAND CRU

Valrhona has created a range of 'grand cru' chocolates from estate-grown cocoa beans where the finest beans are painstakingly selected from plantations spanning the Caribbean to Java (Indonesia). Beans from plantations with a history of quality production will command higher prices in much the same way as domaine cheeses or wines.

GUANAJA, 70 PER CENT COCOA

Made from *trinitario* beans grown in South America, this is the most intense chocolate available; it has a low sugar content and a powerful lingering intensity.

The legendary French restaurateurs, the Troisgros brothers, said of Guanaja: 'An appealing and shiny colour, aromatic strength, and an elegant round and long-lasting taste. This chocolate is a great source of inspiration for our desserts.'

PUR CARAIBE, 66 PER CENT COCOA

Made from pure *trinitario* beans grown in the Caribbean, the taste is reminiscent of dried fruits and vanilla, and woody, like a cask-aged wine.

MANJARI, 64 PER CENT COCOA

Made from *criollo* beans grown on the shores of the Indian ocean, it tastes faintly of flowers and berries with a striking sweet almond after-taste.

SIMON SAYS: WHEN YOU FIRST TASTE THE VERY BEST CHOCOLATE YOU CAN'T HELP BUT NOTICE HOW GOOD IT IS. BUT IT'S NOT UNTIL YOU GO BACK TO THE CHOCOLATE YOU USED TO EAT THAT YOU REALLY DISCOVER THE DIFFERENCE. OTHER CHOCOLATES TASTE OVER-SWEET AND CLOYING ON THE PALATE.

CHOCOLATE SORBET

Philippa Sibley-Cooke | Est Est Est

Serves 6

400 ml water
100 ml milk
130g caster sugar
40g powdered glucose
20g unsweetened cocoa powder
130g Manjari chocolate, finely chopped

Mix together the water, milk, caster sugar, glucose and cocoa powder. Pour the mixture into a saucepan and bring to the boil, whisking occasionally. Place the finely chopped chocolate in a large bowl. Pour the hot mixture onto the chocolate and stir until smooth. Strain through a sieve and allow to cool. Churn in an icecream maker and freeze.

CHOCOLATE AND NOUGAT TARTUFO

Stefano Manfredi | bel mondo

Serves 16

Coconut custard:

1 cup roasted coconut

1200 ml cream

8 egg yolks

200g sugar

Gelato:

1500 ml cream

12 egg yolks

200g honey

100g sugar

Chocolate cream:

200 ml cream

300g best quality milk chocolate, cut into small pieces

Roasted coconut:

4 cups shredded coconut

1/2 cup whole raw peanuts, blanched

1/2 cup whole raw almonds

750g hard Italian torrone (nougat), cut into small dice

TO MAKE THE COCONUT CUSTARD: Add the coconut to the cream in a pan, bring to the boil and set aside for 30 minutes to infuse. Strain through a cloth. Whisk the egg yolks and sugar until the mixture forms ribbons. (When the egg yolks and sugar are beaten they become pale, and when the whisk is drawn across the surface and lifted the beaten mixture falls and resembles a ribbon.)

Add the heated cream and keep whisking until the mixture is smooth. Place over a low heat and stir continuously with a wooden spoon until the custard is thick enough to coat the spoon; this should take 10–15 minutes.

TO MAKE THE GELATO: Heat the cream but do not boil. Whisk the egg yolks, honey and sugar until the mixture forms ribbons. Add the heated cream and keep whisking until the mixture is smooth. Place over a low heat and stir continuously with a wooden spoon until the custard is thick enough to coat the spoon; this should take 10–15 minutes. Transfer immediately to a bowl, then cool and churn in an ice cream maker.

TO MAKE THE CHOCOLATE CREAM: Bring the cream to the boil. Remove from the heat, whisk in the chocolate then set aside to cool.

TO MAKE THE ROASTED COCONUT: Roast the coconut, peanuts and almonds in a preheated 100–120°C oven until they have browned lightly. Set aside to cool.

Add two cups of the roasted coconut and all the nuts and torrone to the chocolate cream and mix thoroughly. Add to the gelato and mix. Spoon the mixture into small individual moulds and freeze overnight. To serve: unmould, roll each tartufo in the remaining coconut and serve with the coconut custard.

ETOILE MOUSSE

Laurent Boillon | Laurent Boulangerie Patisserie
Serves 6

7.5g gelatine leaves
50g Guanaja chocolate
600g thickened cream
150 ml milk

Soften the gelatine leaves in a bowl of cold water. Melt the chocolate in a bowl over a saucepan of boiling water. Whip the cream until soft peaks form. In a separate saucepan heat the milk until it just reaches the boil. Remove from the heat and let stand for 5–10 minutes. Mix the softened gelatine with the hot milk, then slowly add to the melted chocolate. Add a little whipped cream to the mixture and combine well. Softly fold through the remaining cream. Pour into six coffee cups and refrigerate for half an hour until firm. Serve with shaved white chocolate and fresh berries.

TEA & COFFEE

THERE IS NOTHING MORE WELCOMING THAN A KETTLE ON THE BOIL FOR A 'NICE HOT cuppa TEA' OR 'THE AROMA OF FRESHLY brewed COFFEE'; AND IT IS HARD TO IMAGINE LIFE WITHOUT THEM. TEA, THÉ, CHA OR CHAI, WHICH EVER NAME YOU KNOW IT BY, IS THE MOST POPULAR DRINK IN THE WORLD AFTER WATER. WITH ROUGHLY 60 PER CENT LESS caffeine THAN COFFEE, TEA'S MILDLY STIMULATING EFFECTS MEANT THAT IT WAS ORIGINALLY REGARDED AS A MEDICINAL potion. TEA IS SAID TO HAVE BEEN DISCOVERED IN CHINA ABOUT 3000BC — IT SPREAD TO JAPAN AND INDIA, ALTHOUGH IT MOST LIKELY ALREADY EXISTED THERE, AND THEN ON THROUGHOUT THE WORLD. COFFEE HAS ALWAYS BEEN TREASURED FOR ITS STIMULATING EFFECTS. THE coffee TREE APPEARS TO HAVE ORIGINATED IN THE HIGHLANDS OF ETHIOPIA, WHERE THE BEANS APPARENTLY WERE ground (UNROASTED) INTO A PASTE AND EATEN AS A STIMULANT. NO ONE KNOWS HOW OR WHEN THE FIRST COFFEE BEAN CAME TO BE ROASTED, GROUND AND BREWED. COFFEE TREES, HOWEVER, WERE GROWN IN THE MIDDLE EASTERN COUNTRIES BY THE SIXTH CENTURY AD; AND SO IT WAS PROBABLY FIRST MADE IN THE STYLE OF turkish COFFEE — THICK AND GRAINY.

COFFEE

Coffee originated in Ethiopia, where coffee arabica grows wild. It was not until the fifteenth century in southern Arabia that the plant was extensively cultivated. From there it spread to the Mediterranean countries and by the mid-seventeenth century throughout Europe, with coffee-houses springing up in all major cities. In America it supplanted tea as the top beverage after the Boston Tea Party.

There are two major coffee species: *arabica* and *robusta*. *Arabica* is by far the finer of the two. It grows at altitudes of around 1600 m, it is slow growing compared to *robusta*, and the beans develop a richer, more complex flavour; they also contain less than half the caffeine of robusta.

SIMON SAYS: GOOD QUALITY COFFEE IS MADE FROM 100 PER CENT ARABICA BEANS — THERE IS NO SUBSTITUTE.

Robusta coffee plants can be grown in a wider variety of climates than *arabica*, they are more disease resistant and they yield more fruit. They are less aromatic than *arabica* varieties, cheaper to cultivate and are used mostly in instant coffees and as fillers in cheaper coffee blends.

How the beans are roasted will affect their flavour. Roasting can be light, medium or dark (high). The less roasting coffee beans get, the more their flavour will depend upon their intrinsic quality. As a rule, *arabica* beans are not high roasted, but often *robusta* beans are in an attempt to rid the beans of their natural harshness.

THE GRIND

It's important that you grind your coffee to the correct degree for the kind of coffee maker you use. Too fine a grind in a plunger, for example, will make muddy coffee; too coarse a grind in a filter will make weak, tasteless coffee.

TURKISH GRIND: This is almost powdered, the grind for use in an *ibrik*, the long-handled copper jug that is traditional for making strong, sweet Turkish (or Greek) coffee.

VERY FINE GRIND: The grind to use for filtered coffee.

FINE GRIND: This is the one to choose for an espresso machine or the Italian drip pot (Napoletana).

MEDIUM-FINE GRIND: For plunger coffee.

MEDIUM GRIND: For a percolator or the jug method (made in the same way as you make tea, but left to steep for about six minutes before pouring through a strainer).

SERVING COFFEE

Ideally coffee is made with freshly drawn water that is not quite boiling and is served in pre-warmed thick porcelain cups. The following is an explanation of coffee terminology.

CAFÉ AU LAIT: Breakfast coffee in France traditionally served in a bowl. Equal quantities of strong coffee and hot milk.

CAFFE LATTE: One-third espresso to two-thirds hot frothy milk. Usually served in a narrow glass.

ESPRESSO: A small cup (about 30 ml) of very strong black coffee. It is made in an espresso machine that forces steam and boiling water through finely ground coffee, producing a caramel-coloured foam (*crema*) on top of the coffee.

DEMITASSE: This indicates the size of the cup, not the sort of coffee. A demitasse of coffee is a small cup, about the size of an espresso cup, of strong coffee usually served after dinner.

CAPPUCCINO: One-third espresso, one-third hot milk and one-third frothed milk. Powdered chocolate is sprinkled on top.

CAFE CREME: Espresso with hot milk but without the froth (in Australia most of us call this a flat white).

MACCHIATO: Usually served in a small glass, espresso with a dash of foamed milk.

MOCHA: One-third espresso, one-third unsweetened hot chocolate, one-third frothed milk.

RISTRETTO: Same amount of coffee as espresso, but less water; an extra strong espresso.

DOPPIO: A double espresso.

LONG BLACK: Espresso made with three times the usual amount of water.

ROMANO: Espresso served with a twist of lemon.

IRISH COFFEE: Strong coffee laced with Irish whisky and topped with a layer of cream (pour it over the back of a spoon so it floats on the surface).

VIENNA COFFEE: A strong brew topped with sweetened whipped cream.

TURKISH OR GREEK COFFEE: made in an *ibrik*, a small copper pot with a long handle. It is extremely strong and usually drunk very sweet in tiny cups, accompanied by a glass of iced water.

SIMON SAYS: MILKY COFFEES SUCH AS CAFÉ AU LAIT AND CAFFE LATTE ARE TRADITIONALLY DRUNK IN THE MORNING. THAT IS BECAUSE MILKY COFFEE IS HARD TO DIGEST, ESPECIALLY AFTER A MEAL.

STORING COFFEE

Once coffee has been roasted it shouldn't be kept for long — the essential oils that give coffee its flavour begin to evaporate. Buy only enough coffee beans to last two weeks and store in an airtight container in the refrigerator.

The flavour of ground coffee lasts even less time, so try to grind your coffee freshly each time you make it. If you buy it ground, store in the refrigerator in an airtight container for no more than a week.

TEA

A native of India, China and Japan, tea was brought to the Continent by the Dutch in 1610, and reached England in 1644. The Dutch added a dash of milk to their cups and the English took to this way of serving it with alacrity. There are more than 3000 varieties of tea, most taking their names from the regions where they are grown.

High quality tea is a new concept for most Australians. While we take the trouble to grind our coffee beans just before using them and we're fussy about the blend, we're quite happy to buy a brand of tea

MARIAGE FRÈRES

Henri and Edouard Mariage founded the Mariage Frères tea company in Paris in 1854. They were descended from a long line of tea traders, beginning in 1660 when Nicolas Mariage made several voyages to Persia and the East Indies on behalf of King Louis XIV and the French East India Company. Henri and Edouard bought tea from China and Ceylon and supplied it to hotels, tea rooms, delicatessens and exclusive retailers. After 130 years Mariage Frères decided to open to the public; they now supply tea grown in 32 different countries and as well as their original headquarters in the historic Marais district of Paris, they have a boutique on the Left Bank and several tea houses in Japan.

that could be a blend of 20 or 30 different teas of varying quality without a notion of what kind of tea we're drinking. Or we put a tea bag into a mug and pour boiling water over it.

So what is it that makes the difference between a high quality tea and the ordinary, commercial tea we buy in our supermarkets? The best tea is single-estate tea, i.e. it is not blended with other teas but comes from one tea garden, usually situated at a high altitude. Even though all tea is derived from the same evergreen plant, *Camellia sinensis*, its flavour varies according to the region in which it was grown and after which it tends to be named, so a Darjeeling tea has quite a different taste from an Assam tea. The time of harvesting is important, too — first flush, i.e. spring harvest, has a lighter taste than the more mature second and autumnal flushes. The way the tea is processed will also affect its taste. Black tea is fully fermented and has a completely different taste from unfermented green tea or semi-fermented Oolong tea. Tea tasters from the great tea companies judge the

quality of the tea on the appearance and aroma of the dried and infused leaf, the colour of the tea and, finally, on the taste.

However there are good quality blended teas too. Commercial teas can be a blend of as many as 30 different teas and cheap teas, known as fillers, are often added.

SIMON SAYS GOOD TEA BLENDS ARE MADE UP OF QUALITY TEA LEAVES, AND FILLERS AREN'T USED — THERE'S A WORLD OF DIFFERENCE IN THE TASTE.

TEA TERMS

Teas are classified according to their country of origin or by smaller districts within those countries, such as Darjeeling. There's a lot of confusion about the terms used to describe grades of tea. People often think that orange pekoe means the tea has an orange flavour, and that flowery orange pekoe describes a scented tea. But these terms simply describe the size of the leaf.

Orange pekoe (OP) is characterised by long leaves rolled lengthways like needles. These leaves are picked when the terminal bud has developed into a leaf and the tea rarely contains tips. Flowery orange pekoe (FOP) refers to the terminal bud and first leaf of each shoot. These young tender leaves make a lovely tea.

Even finer teas are made from golden flowery orange pekoe (GFOP), tippy golden flowery orange pekoe (TGFOP) and finest tippy golden flowery orange pekoe (FTGFOP), culminating in special finest tippy golden flowery orange pekoe (SFTGFOP). These last ones are quite rare and very expensive.

Broken-leaf tea is simply tea with leaves that have been broken, and tea fannings are leaves that are broken even more: into tiny flat pieces about 1.5 mm long.

GREEN TEA

Green tea is unfermented. In Japanese green tea, the most famous of which is Sencha, the leaves are sweated in a steam tank until they become soft enough to roll. They are partially rolled by hand and then dried. The process is repeated several times and is highly labour intensive, which is why Japanese green tea is so expensive.

It's important to use water at the correct temperature for green tea; pouring boiling water over it can destroy its flavour. Some teas require water at 70°C, others at 50°C, so check the labels. Green tea has a clean, fresh flavour and is best sipped from small, handleless china cups.

MAKING TEA

There's some difference of opinion about the boiling water issue. Our mothers taught us to warm the pot, bring the water to the boil, and immediately pour the water onto the tea in the pot. The water should never be boiled for more than a few seconds or it loses its 'sparkle'. The dictum was clear: take the pot to the kettle, not the kettle to the pot, so that the water is truly boiling as you pour it out.

However, French tea company Mariage Frères suggest the water should be barely simmering when it is poured over the tea leaves. Extended boiling, they say, 'kills' the water and damages tea leaves, harming both aroma and flavour.

The amount of tea to use depends upon taste. The rule has always been, 'one [teaspoon] for each person and one for the pot'. But when using high quality teas you will probably use less, depending upon the tea you've chosen.

EVERYONE AGREES UPON CERTAIN THINGS:

Tea tastes better in fine china tea cups and it stays hot longer, and it's a good idea to warm the cups first with hot water.

Tea should be kept hot while it's steeping: cover the pot with a tea cosy or use a well-insulated pot.

If you use two or three types of tea, especially if they're quite different in flavour, such as black tea, green tea and smoky tea, use a different teapot for each type to keep the flavours separate.

For flavoured teas and herb teas, glass teapots are recommended because they don't retain odours and you can change from one

flavour to another without fear of mingling their taste.

Tea tastes better if made from water that is not chlorinated; use bottled spring water in preference to tap water.

Store tea in an airtight caddy in a cool dry place out of the way of stronger aromas such as coffee and spices.

THE ETIQUETTE OF TEA

Milk in first or milk in last? There used to be an English expression, 'she's rather MIF' (milk in first), meaning she's not quite up to scratch socially; society dictated the milk was added after the tea was poured. Despite this, tea connoisseurs agree that tea tastes better if you pour the milk into your cup first. The milk 'cooks' slightly when the hot tea is poured over it, giving it a more blended taste.

Some teas should be drunk black: the delicate, subtle taste of whole-leaf tea can be best appreciated when drunk without milk, sugar or lemon. Scented teas such as Earl Grey are best drunk black too, and you should never add milk to green tea. But blended teas, such as English Breakfast, benefit from a drop or two of cold milk.

THE MARIAGE FRÈRES METHOD OF MAKING TEA
1 Preheat the teapot by rinsing with boiling water.
2 Add the appropriate amount of tea per person and let the leaves stand for a few minutes to allow the steam to begin developing the aroma.
3 Pour hot water onto the tea.
4 Let the tea steep.
5 Stir the tea and serve.

Mariage Frères suggest using a teapot with a built-in strainer to hold the leaves, which is rinsed with boiling water before use and removed before the tea is stirred and poured. They also believe that their teas should not be drunk too hot or the subtle fragrances won't be appreciated.

INDEX